The Road Too Far

For Sarah
Best wishes.
Lester McNall

THE ROAD TOO FAR

The Road Too Far

Lester McNall

This book is based on the diary of Eileen Jobe Pickens and the journal of Marie McNall. All the characters were real people and events occurred as described.

Copyright © 2019 by Lester R. McNall

Cover design by SelfPubBookCovers.com/RLSather

d

The book is dedicated to the memory of the six travelers, all now deceased. Each of them played a role in my early life and will always occupy a special place in my heart.

Also a tribute to all the kind folks who helped them along the way.

The author wishes to acknowledge the contributions of:

Randine Jaastad Larson for encouraging pursuit of this project and for locating and providing Marie's journal and letters.

Vickie Robbins Bailey and Carol Dallas for help with proofing and editing.

Jaime Tirado for Spanish translations.

Joe VanZandt for photos of Pershing Pickens.

Jan Sheafor for providing photos taken on the trip.

e

Contents

THE ROAD TOO FAR

h

Chapter 1: Introductions

<u>Rivas, Nicaragua. Tuesday, May 25, 1948.</u> *Invierno*, the rainy season, had begun and would continue until October. The rain was not incessant but came in brief showers punctuated with occasional heavy downpours. Unpaved streets and roads, and there were quite a few in and around Rivas, soon became impassable quagmires. This included the driveway to Dr. Alfonso Rivas's ranch house. He would have dental patients waiting in his office in town, so he decided to ride his horse to work again this day rather than risk getting stuck in the mud with his car.

On the way to his office he decided to have a cup of coffee at the Gran Central Hotel. Something odd caught his eye as he approached the hotel: two black vehicles parked in front. Although caked with mud, he could tell they were 1948 model Chevrolets, the first new American cars he had seen since the war; a sedan with a license plate that read "WISCONSIN. America's Dairyland" and a panel truck with Indiana plates. *"Alguien esta muy lejos de casa"*, he thought to himself: "Someone's a long way from home".

He finished his coffee and, as he was leaving, he was approached in the lobby by a woman who appeared to be in her early fifties. From her looks, dress, and manner, he judged her to be American. "Pardon me, sir," she said, "but do you speak English?" "Yes, I do," he replied. "Can I help you in any way?" "Well, we're travelers driving through and we're trying to get to *San Juan del Sur* to catch a boat. It looks as if we may be stranded here for a while and we could use some help with translations and some advice on how best to proceed". "It would be an honor for me to assist you in any way that I can" was his welcomed reply.

She introduced herself. Her name was Jessie Pickens, although everyone called her Babe. She was traveling with her son Pershing, his wife Eileen, Babe's 25-year old daughter Marietta, her cousin Janet, and their friend

1

Marie.

Dr. Rivas identified himself as a dentist specializing in orthodontics. He was born and raised here in Rivas but had attended dental college in the U.S. He lived on the Rivas family ranch outside the town with his wife Hortensia and seven children.

As the two were talking, they were joined by Marie and Eileen who were ready to go shopping. Introductions were made all around. At about the same time Johnny Rivas, the doctor's oldest son, age 22, arrived on the scene. He was especially delighted to meet Marie and was eager to escort the ladies around town. Dr. Rivas rode off to his office on his horse. Persh soon joined the shoppers downtown where they found nothing they wanted to buy, so later they stopped at Dr. Rivas's office to change some dollars into *cordobas,* the Nicaraguan currency. After lunch at the hotel they picked up Dr. Rivas and drove out to look at the road to *San Juan del Sur.* It looked questionable and was reported to be impassable in certain spots along its nearly 20-mile route; also there was a river that had to be forded. Pic and Jan had by now returned from taking the early morning train to *San Juan del Sur* to check on road conditions at that end. Their assessment was not encouraging.

In this short time it had become apparent that Dr. Rivas had bonded with the group and was ready and willing to take them  under his wing. Their youthfulness and spirit of adventure brought excitement into his humdrum existence. Also, it would enhance his prestige in the community to be seen as the leader, protector, and advisor to this mysterious group of Americans who had dropped in as if from a distant planet. Of course the pretty girls added to the attraction.

They accepted Dr. Rivas's invitation to come to his ranch for dinner, piled into the two vehicles and headed out. The truck got stuck in mud at the gate. They were able to push it out but decided it was best to leave the autos and walk to the house from the gate. They trudged through mud in the dark to reach the house which seemed rather insubstantial by American standards. The house was so dimly illuminated inside that Eileen called it "*dark and dreary, like something out of Inner Sanctum*". They were served eggs that were unappetizing, cold rice, dry beans, and coffee, thick as mud, in tin cups. The group was glad they had brought dysentery pills with them. Still, they appreciated the hospitality of the doctor and allowed for the fact that the cook had no advance warning to prepare food for such a crowd. They felt sufficiently ill-at-ease that they declined the doctor's invitation to stay overnight at the ranch. But though the meal left something to be desired, the liquor was good. As they sat for after-dinner drinks by lamplight they told the Rivas family the story of their trip.

Chapter 2: GettingReady

The plan was to drive from Wisconsin to Santiago, Chile, on the Pan American Highway. The concept of a road to connect all the Americas was conceived in 1923 but took form slowly. Some progress was made in the 1930s but development was expedited by WWII as shipping by sea became more hazardous. An article in Popular Mechanics magazine in 1946 predicted that the road from Alaska to Chile would be completed by 1948. Perhaps this article inspired Pershing Pickens to seriously consider making such a trip. If so, he may have overlooked the paragraph in the magazine article that mentioned that the weak link in the highway was in Central America; fewer than 30% of all roads there were paved.

Persh was 29 and less than a year out of the U.S. Navy where he had been a Lieutenant. He had flown a scout bomber off the aircraft carrier USS Franklin (Big Ben). During the Battle for Leyte Gulf off the Philippines on October 24, 1944, he single-handedly sank the Japanese destroyer Wakaba and was awarded the Distinguished Flying Cross. He now lived on the small family farm in Cloverdale, Indiana. He was an outdoorsman who disdained the norms of society, loved guns, game hunting, and traveling in the pursuit of wildlife. He provided some income by capturing exotic animals and selling them to zoos in the U.S. His wife, Eileen, worked in an office in Indianapolis and shared his interests in travel and hunting.

His young sister Marietta, who everybody called Pic, could well have been described as a tomboy, a girl whose actions and activities were not limited by her gender. At age 25, she was a beautiful young lady with an easygoing manner, an endearing personality, and unlimited interests. She and her mother, Babe, had lived and worked in upstate New York during the war. When the war ended, they returned to their home base in Janesville, Wisconsin, where Pic joined up with her cousin, Janet McCartney.

Jan and her friend, Marie McNall, were both farm girls who had been classmates at Janesville High. After graduating in 1941, they moved to Madison and, during the war years, worked the swing shift at Ray-O-Vac where batteries for the Army Signal Corps were made. The two had just returned in late 1946 from a two-year stint in Rome, Italy, working for the U.S. Overseas Liquidation Agency, a temporary organization that had been established to dispose of military material left in Europe. So the taste of adventure was in their mouths.

Persh had already bought a panel truck and was outfitting it in Indiana for such a trip. Pic liked Persh's idea of driving to South America and persuaded Jan and Marie to join in the venture. Their idea was to buy a car and follow the truck in a caravan. Instead of just talking about it, they made plans to do it. To earn money, the girls bought 500 baby turkey chicks, raised them to maturity, and delivered them oven-ready to customers in the

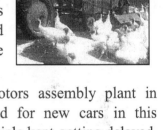

Madison area for Thanksgiving 1947. They greatly underestimated the amount of labor required but, with the unrecompensed assistance and long hours of toil from every friend, relative, and acquaintance who could be cajoled into helping, the project was a success.

A new car was ordered from the General Motors assembly plant in Janesville. Due to the extremely heavy demand for new cars in this immediate post-war period, delivery of their vehicle kept getting delayed. Marie was personally acquainted with Mr. Markham, the plant manager, and was able to get him to intercede on their behalf. The girls took possession of a black four-door Chevrolet Fleetline sedan in February 1948. They planned to sell the car once they arrived in Santiago and use the money to pay for their return trip back to the States.

Chapter 3: Journey to the Mexican Border

Preparations had been under way for weeks. Last minute activities centered on getting the cars ready, deciding what to take, and final packing. Marie typed a list of everything she was taking in her baggage which consisted of a small suitcase, a large suitcase, a make-up kit, a sewing box, two cameras, and a writing portfolio.

They left Janesville on Thursday, April 8, 1948, the three girls in the car, the others in the truck. In addition to clothes and everyday necessities, they took a good supply of cheap costume jewelry, knick-knacks, and cigarettes to use as barter. Each person had their own compartment in the truck, a sturdy box in which to keep their personal belongings. By the time they said their good-byes, took pictures, and had some farewell toasts, it was 3:40 p.m. when they finally departed. A friend had given them a gallon jug of red wine to take along on the road. The truck odometer read 2,908 miles.

South of Rockford, they viewed the huge stone statue of Indian Chief Blackhawk overlooking the Rock River, then stopped for a bite to eat at Viola, Illinois. They spent their first night on the road at a gas station in Quincy, Illinois. The initial camp-out was rather trying as the night was cold, and comfort among the suitcases and compartments was at a minimum. The wine helped serve as a sleep-aid. Pic, Jan, Babe, and Marie slept in the truck and said *"it wasn't bad but got rather stuffy before morning"*.

On Friday they drove southwest through Missouri, celebrating Babe's 51st birthday with lunch at Lake of the Ozarks. Their destination that day was Savoy, a small town just west of Fayetteville, Arkansas, where friends of Eileen lived. Here the group split up. The three girls drove the car south to Denton, Texas, north of Dallas, where they had friends to visit. The others stayed in Savoy with Eileen's friends through the weekend.

Persh and some boys went fox hunting, set fish lines, and gathered mushrooms. The girls couldn't find a place to stay in Denton so drove on to Dallas and had to wait until 5:00 a.m. to get a room in a motor court.

Tuesday, April 13. The truck left Arkansas and drove through picturesque hilly and green country to join the girls in Dallas. Marie had gone ahead to Austin in the car to spend some time with Steve, an Army lieutenant she had met in Italy and had almost married; he was now a civilian attending the University of Texas Law School. Persh and Eileen stopped at a Sears store in north Dallas and bought a block and tackle, water bags, tin cups, and oil.

They arrived in Austin about noon on Wednesday to pick up Marie and the car and decided to stay in tourist cabins in Austin overnight. On Thursday they met Steve at Marie's hotel and did some shopping in Austin, then drove on to San Antonio where they all slept in the truck near a tourist camp north of the city. Friday morning they played the role of tourists: visits to the zoo, the Chinese Sunken Garden, the Alamo. They each bought a hammock with mosquito netting anticipating hot, humid nights in the tropics. That evening they continued on to a roadside park just north of Laredo where they fell asleep to the sound of howling coyotes.

While the girls slept in on Saturday morning, Persh and Eileen strolled through the surrounding desert where they enjoyed seeing lizards, cacti, and desert birds. The group rented cabins at the nearby Ranch Motel, then went into Laredo, stopped by AAA for maps and travel advice, shopped for food, and later cooked steaks at the roadside park. On Sunday, the girls sunned themselves while Persh took the car, then the truck, to be greased. The day was capped off by crossing the border for dinner at the legendary Cadillac Bar in Nuevo Laredo. *"Quite expensive!"*

Persh had brought along a Smith & Wesson 0.38 Special revolver, so at 8 a.m. Monday they went to see the Mexican Consul about getting a gun permit and transient cards. The consul told Persh to contact a Mexican General in Nuevo Laredo who at first refused to grant a permit but, after giving Persh some paperwork to fill out and keeping him waiting for more than an hour, reconsidered, and the permit was issued. Persh felt the delay could have been avoided if the consul had walked him through the protocol and provided the forms required for the permit.

The next day was spent in preparation for border crossing: a visit to Dr. Lowry, recommended by AAA, to get tetanus and typhus shots and prescriptions for several drugs that might be needed along the way; a trip to the drug store to get the prescriptions filled. Jan had some dental work done. They bought six sturdy metal 5-gallon gas cans (one for water, one for white gas for the Coleman stove and lantern), cleaned and filled the cans, got first aid supplies, went to AAA for insurance on the cars. This was followed by grocery shopping, after which steaks were again cooked at the roadside park on a perfect moonlit night. Pic and Jan climbed an orange tree and picked a few oranges but they were very sour.

Wednesday, April 21. They got up early to finish packing, fueled the vehicles and then drove to AAA to change dollars to pesos. There they learned they had to fill out forms to register all foreign-made articles. When they ate lunch at a drugstore counter they figured it would be their last decent meal for quite a while. After some last minute shopping for more groceries, they headed for the International Bridge and whatever lay ahead.

Chapter 4: Traveling To Mexico City

They crossed the border at 1:05 p.m. on Wednesday, April 21---a beautiful day; blue sky with soft white clouds. Border officials asked only for their transient visas and car documents and instructed them to stop for inspection before 2:00 p.m. at the next station fourteen miles ahead. Everyone at that inspection station was polite, respectful, and spoke some English. An old man wrote a note welcoming them to Mexico. A superficial inspection took about 45 minutes as two men took the baggage out and a woman checked the suitcases, boxes, and compartments. Persh tipped them 10 pesos and the travelers departed, heading south on Highway 85 amongst burros, peons, and goats. The road beckoned as if inviting them to the wondrous views and adventures that lay ahead. The highway was paved, in good condition, and ran straight as an arrow for 45 miles. Flat uninhabited plains were covered with cacti in bloom—orange, red, and yellow. At *Sabinas Hidalgo*, a former mining town, they stopped for refreshments at Power's restaurant and appreciated the clean, comfortable restrooms. A very long and winding road took them across *Mamulique Pass*, El. 2,280 ft., then soon brought them to another inspection station where they expected to have to unload everything again, but this inspection was perfunctory. A civilian who worked for the government gave them helpful information, recommended places to eat, and gave them a card of introduction to a man at the Chapultepec Hotel in Mexico City. The terrain became more mountainous as they were now in the Sierra Madre range. They were very impressed by a large mountain, *Cerro Tia Chena*, El. 8,858 ft., looming ahead north of *Monterrey*.

The view coming into *Monterrey*[2] was beautiful, the city surrounded by mountains with Saddle Mountain (*Cerro de la Silla*) on the left. North of town they were impressed by the pretty homes and numerous nice-looking motor courts. *Monterrey* struck them as being a very attractive city with a lot of industry. There were many large manufacturing plants including

Cuauhtémoc, the largest brewery in Mexico (Dos Equis, Carta Blanca, Bohemia). The two cars got briefly separated while looking for gas but met at the south edge of the city where they bought their first "liters". AAA had advised buying Mexolina, the Mexican premium gas with an octane rating of 72, equivalent to regular American gas, as compared to Mexican regular with an octane rating of 57. There were more fine-looking homes south of town. It was almost dark when they entered the twenty-mile stretch of lovely, but narrow, *Huajuco Canyon*, filled with orange groves and splendid homes. A big black cloud started forming, then many more, and the wind blew furiously through the canyon. At *Villa de Santiago* a few miles further down the road they passed through what seemed to be a twilight zone where time had stood still, where customs seemed not to have changed for centuries. The land was hilly with sparse vegetation except for an occasional orange grove. They now saw burros, horses, steers, and herds of goats as well as oxen pulling carts. The greatest menace to safe driving seemed to be the animals that freely roamed the countryside. The roadside was dotted with odd little houses of rock and stone with thatched roofs. They drove another ten miles before they decided to set up camp at 8:00 p.m. atop a large hill on a curve north of *Ciudad de Allende*. Everyone was tired and hungry. They unloaded the truck, ate spam sandwiches, green beans, and coffee. The beds had to be remade as customs inspectors had dismantled them. They all slept in the truck. The night was warm, everybody was restless, and no one got much sleep. Eileen complained that Marie snuggled so close to her she could hardly move.

They were awakened at 6:15 a.m. with a serenade by a *muchacho* coming down a path, riding one burro and leading another one. He alternated between singing loudly and playing a piccolo. Persh greeted him with "Buenos Dias" and received "Hello, Sir" in reply. The boy crossed the highway and wandered on up the mountain where cows were grazing. After the necessary little side trips they were off to *Montemorelos*, located in a fruit-growing area. The road was lined with one fruit stand after the other. They found a stand that had an interpreter and bought two dozen grapefruit, two dozen oranges, and forty tangerines for 6.75 pesos (US$1.35). The interpreter told them that the best fruit from the area was

shipped to Canada. They bought the last eight eggs in a grocery store, then looked for a place to stop and eat breakfast. They passed through *Linares*, quite a large town with odd little shops that had no signs on them; one had to look inside to see whether it was a home or a store and what they sold.

Around *Linares,* center of the orange-belt region, fruit grew in profusion: navel oranges, lemons, mangos, prickly pears, papayas, guavas, figs, cherimoyas, and others. Farming and ranchland began to appear; oxen and tractors were both being used for plowing. South of *Linares* they found a place to fix breakfast, built a wood fire, cooked hash and eggs and brewed

coffee. As they were ready to leave, they discovered that Pic had left the key to the lock on the gas cap of the car at the fruit stand in *Montemorelos*, so Pic, Jan, and Babe were dispatched back thirty miles to look for it. During the three-hour wait for them to return

with the key, two hombres came along the road, their oxen and cart loaded with cactus leaves. They waved and exchanged greetings as they slowly rumbled by. A big dog and a goat visited them. Marie spread a newspaper on the ground and wrote in her journal.

As they continued the country now became hilly and looked quite tropical with a steady increase in the density and variety of vegetation. The towering Sierra Madre Mountains to the right formed a majestic background. Several magnificent huge churches came into view. The road climbed up into *Ciudad Victoria* which lies in a valley between flat mesas thickly covered with underbrush. *Victoria* is the capital of *Tamaulipas* and is the center for some of the best fishing and hunting in Mexico. South of

Victoria, the road dropped again and 24 miles later, at 6:15 p.m., they crossed the *Tropic of Cancer*[3] thereby officially entering the tropics. After a three mile climb up the *Mesa de Llera*, they stopped to enjoy the splendid view. Looking for a place to settle down for the night, they came upon the *Rio Guayalejo,* a river with a bed 1,000 feet wide which was practically dry. They drove across the dry bed to camp by a small residual stream, but the sky became very dark with black clouds. Having read that the  river could become a raging torrent during a rainstorm, they decided to camp nearer the road. The gas stove didn't work well so they built a wood fire and ate spaghetti and meat balls. That night they all slept in the truck without getting much sleep due to mosquitos, the heat, and intermittent rain. They were all bitten by some insect whose bite caused swelling on their arms, legs, and faces. They would awaken, eat tangerines, spray themselves against the insects, then try to get back to sleep.

Back on the road next morning, the countryside looked distinctly tropical with bananas, palm trees, Spanish moss, colorful birds, and gorgeous butterflies of green, yellow, black, and delicate blue. Around *Ciudad Mante* they saw irrigated crops---40,000 acres of sugarcane to supply the largest sugar refinery in Mexico. When they stopped for gas at *Ciudad Valles*, Babe bought some topaz and aquamarine stones from a persistent peddler. They searched for the local icehouse, eventually found it identified by a sign that said "Alaska", then encountered some language difficulties in getting their rusty water can filled and purchasing a bottle of distilled water for the car batteries. They had been cautioned about drinking the water in countries south of the border so they relied on colas, juices, and beer to keep them hydrated for most of the trip.

After leaving *Valles,* they entered *Huasteca*[4] Indian country and found that the Indians weren't nearly as friendly as the Mexicans. This Indian region had been inaccessible until the highway was built in 1936. Many of the people knew no Spanish, only their native language, and lived as they had for generations. This area was very picturesque, their huts built from the native bamboo with palm thatching. Mistletoe, orchids, and other parasitic plants grew in the trees. It was quite mountainous here with fields of bananas growing on the mountain sides in rows reaching all the way to the top. It was amazing to see how the land could be cleared, planted, and the trees tended and harvested on such steep slopes.

They finally agreed to humor Babe's insistence on a side trip, so three miles south of *Huichihuayan*, they left the highway and took a gravel road to the west. They were looking for a place to camp but there was none to be found before they came to a stream which had to be crossed by ferry. The ferry in this case was a raft powered by ropes pulled by several men on each side of the stream. After watching a large bus cross, they felt it was safe for their heavily loaded truck so it went first, then the car with the girls.

There were steep inclines in the road on both sides of the approach to the boat which caused some sweaty palms but were navigated without incident. Persh paid the ferry one peso for both cars. Now they began to climb a very narrow, winding road. At this point Babe decided she would stop reading about side trips. Eileen admitted to being scared *"as the road was so narrow with so many bends you couldn't see around or pass anyone"*. They resorted to blowing the horn on the curves. The few pullout areas looked as if they wouldn't support the weight of a car, but they used one to ponder the fact that the bus that had crossed on the ferry just before them would be coming back down at some point. They finally arrived at a slightly flat place having a small settlement. Marie got her Spanish book out and approached a cute Indian girl standing in a schoolyard to ask if the bus came back down that night. They both chattered away, making gestures with both hands while the rest of the group chimed in with questions and Spanish words they hurriedly looked up in a book. After about ten minutes

Marie decided that the bus would come down later that night so they bravely resumed climbing further up until they found a place to pull off the road where they thought they would be quite isolated. But when Marie and Eileen sought a secluded area to squat, they found little bamboo huts everywhere. When the girls started fixing dinner, people appeared from all over the hillside. Gradually the Indians became braver and bolder, especially the men, and soon several men were right up there with them. Not knowing whether they were welcome or not, the travelers smiled bravely, tried to talk to them, and gave them cigarettes. Eventually everything settled down and the men left, but children and women continued to peek at them. Marie and Jan slept in the car, Pic and Babe in the truck seats. Persh and Eileen slept in hammocks with people passing by all night. Eileen complained that the moon was so bright she couldn't sleep. They both felt cold so they built a fire to warm up and dry out from the cold damp air. They had no more than got back to sleep when the morning traffic on the path began.

Next morning, breakfast was prepared and eaten with all the foot traffic going by; the natives were greeted with "Buenos Dias" to which the men replied but not the women. After breakfast, their climb up the mountain was resumed. Eileen described it as *"quite a trip, more than I expected, winding, winding, and winding up and around, passing huts and little stores along the mountain"*. After climbing to 3,200 ft., they arrived at the village of *Xilitla* where they found an old man who spoke some English. They were told that the road was constructed entirely by the natives, literally carving it out of the mountain including a small tunnel. He told them about the old church, how the town was completely destroyed at one time, when people came back there were "tigers" living in the church, and there was a cave down below in which parakeets lived. As they started back down the mountain they found the cave and explored it a bit. They saw a few birds and several huge black spiders. Their side trip concluded as they descended the mountain, re-crossed the stream on that ferry, rejoined the highway and continued on to *Tamazumchale* where they stopped for gas. Just south of there, the road climbed terrifically and then descended into *Jacala,* a very attractive village. They had a wonderful view as the road dropped down into it, then ascended again into *Los Marmoles*, a magnificent gorge (later declared a national park), very scenic and very deep. They found a suitable high place that was pleasantly cool on which to camp. As they were eating dinner they noticed two pigs, then a little boy, dirty and shabbily dressed in scant clothing. He looked frozen, sat and watched them eat. They gave him crackers, and Marie tried to talk with him. When his brother appeared with a little sister, they gave the boys a few centavos and they left. Everybody retired early with a lovely moon popping up over the mountains.

Sunday, April 25. As they were preparing to leave their campsite, another little boy appeared with his mother, wanting something but unable to communicate. Eileen gave the mother forty centavos and she left. From the gorge, they descended into cactus country. Fields and fields of *maguey* (century plants), the fiber used to make many things, the sap fermented to make *pulque*, an alcoholic beverage. On the road were Indians loaded with wood, roosters, pigs; there were little burros carrying rope, fiber, cloth, all going to the open-air market in *Zimapan*. They drove past the market without stopping but could see fruits and brightly colored cloth made from maguey on display. On the south edge of town they stopped for gas at a filling station that surprised them with neat, clean restrooms and friendly servicemen in crisp white uniforms. The highway now alternated between climbing mountains, then descending to lowlands full of cactus. They again encountered people on the road heading for next day's market in *Ixmiquilpan*, the center of maguey production. On the way to *Actopan*, they saw fields of wheat and corn, bales of hay, straw stacks, sheep and goats. High on a nearby mountaintop there appeared to be the ruins of an old church but in reality it was just a natural stone outcropping. After *Actopan* the highway climbed to more than 8,000 feet, the highest point on their journey so far, near *Pachuca*, an old mining town. As they approached

Mexico City, the land became very flat and they got their first glimpse of the two snow-capped volcanoes, *Popocatépetl* and *Ixtaccihuatl*, both more than 17,000 feet high. Now there was more traffic on the road including a sporting group riding bicycles. About fifteen miles outside the city, they stopped to cook a meal they called breakfast even though it was lunchtime then motored on into Mexico City arriving at 2:00 p.m.

Chapter 5: Two Nights In Mexico City

They rented cabins at Sunset Courts, a Triple-A-recommended motor court, and rushed to the bull fights at *Rancho del Charro*. There were six fights, and they watched with excitement as one matador was knocked down four times, but he was not badly injured. Afterwards they returned to their cabins, had dinner, then drove around the city for a while, but the traffic and the wild drivers soon wore them down so they returned to their cabins to get a good night's rest.

Monday, April 26. In the morning they visited the U.S. Embassy for information and to pick up mail, then to the Guatemalan Consul for tourist cards, and a wire was sent requesting permission to bring the gun into Guatemala. A visit was made to AAA, then to Western Union where wires were sent back home, then to the Post Office to buy airmail stamps. They lunched at Sanborn's Restaurant, then rushed to the San Juan Market but the businesses inside the market were closed. They drove around looking for Chapultepec Castle where Emperor Maximilian had lived but never found it.

Back at the cabins, Pic announced that she and Jan had dates with the 1st and 2nd Vice Consuls from the Embassy. The dates arrived with two other men, so Marie and Babe joined the party. Persh and Eileen took a cab to the *Reforma*, had a beer (for thirty cents) at Ciro's, another at the Broadway Bar, and one at a cute hole-in-the-wall. They then walked back to the cabins, arriving after midnight to locked gates so had to ring for the night watchman to let them in. The girls returned at 3:30 a.m. after a wonderful evening of sightseeing, dinner, and dancing. For them it had been a night of the best of everything; for the married couple, a night of slumming.

Chapter 6: On To Puebla and Oaxaca

<u>Tuesday, April 27.</u> The girls were ready to go by 9:00 a.m. They rushed to have breakfast at the court, packed, and checked out before noon but then hung around for lunch. They found an American grocery store, bought corned beef and wieners, finally found their way out of town at 6:00 p.m. but forgot to gas up before they left. They drove through very flat country for a while, through tiny Indian villages with a strong wind blowing dust across the plains. The road narrowed with tall trees on both sides, becoming so narrow that semi-trucks had hit about one out of every six trees. The road became very steep and winding as it climbed the mountains and took them toward the snow-capped volcanoes. Looking back there was a wonderful view of the basin that was once Lake Texcoco[5]. The sun on the mountains and the dust in the sky gave a prismatic effect resulting in a gorgeous array of colors. At 7:30 p.m., at an elevation of 10,000 ft., they stopped and ate corned beef sandwiches and soup. Pic wasn't feeling well and didn't eat. The air turned quite chilly before they bedded down for the night at 9:15.

The next day dawned clear, bright, and frigid after a night with a moon so bright it hurt the eyes to look at it. Everyone had been cold during the night. Jan found ice in the water bag. There was ice along the roadside as they climbed higher still to cross the Continental Divide at 10,486 ft. At *Rio Frito de Juarez* the volcanoes were so near it seemed one could reach out and touch them. They stopped there for gas and eggs and to enjoy the view. Smoke was rising from *Popocatépetl*. They had breakfast and took some pictures.

In *Huejotzingo* there were several stands selling woolen goods. After some dickering, Eileen purchased a large, striped blanket for 22 pesos. From

Huejotzingo a large mountain, *La Malinche,* could be seen and on its summit was said to be a profile of the Indian wife of Cortez[7]. *Cholula,* the next town, was once the center of the Toltec kingdom and had a population of 100,000 and more than 400 temples when Cortez destroyed it in 1519 in a ruthless massacre of innocent people. The town is built around the *Pyramid of Quetzalcoatl* (Great Pyramid of Cholula), said to be the largest pyramid in the world by volume. The great pyramid now resembled a huge hill as it had become covered with earth and overgrown with vegetation. Excavations had revealed a honeycomb of passages, galleries, stairways, many relics, and burial sites. Atop the pyramid was the *Iglesia de Nuestra Senora de los Remedios* (Church of the Virgin of Remedies) built by the Spaniards in 1666. Jan took a picture of it. The market there had tomatoes and bolts of cloth.

Cholula borders *Puebla (Puebla de Zaragoza),* the fourth largest city in Mexico and important in Mexican history [6]. Upon entering the city, the travelers were approached by a young man who offered to escort them to places of interest. His name was Jose, 20 years old and a licensed guide, so they hired him. Their first stop was at an onyx factory where Eileen bought a small dog and Persh got a large mounted onyx tiger, then to a silver store where Marie paid 75 pesos (US$15) for a silver necklace and bracelet. Then to the Convent (*El Convento de Santa Mónica*) where Jose relished relating its somewhat lurid history. In 1857, Reform Laws were passed in Mexico that abolished monasteries and convents, but this convent continued in secret operation underground for more than 75 years. It was located across the street from a police station. In 1935 a policeman accidentally knocked over a flower pot and discovered a hidden button underneath. When he pressed it, a Sister opened a secret door and the clandestine convent was exposed. The youngest nun was 65, the oldest in her 90s. A family had lived in the front of the building and protected the secret although suspicions had been aroused because people wondered at the large amount of food that was delivered to the house. The visitors saw the robes the nuns wore, scratchy wool with no underwear, barbed head gears to torture themselves. They dressed in the dark as they weren't permitted to see naked bodies. The head Sister slept on a board. If one sinned, their hands were tied and they had to lap their food like an animal. Their living quarters were beneath a charming church, and there were secret peepholes so they could witness Mass above. There was a room where one was put alone to die. There were burial tombs and a pit full of skulls. On display were some weird artifacts: a preserved heart and a dried tongue. These were offset by some interesting paintings, several on velvet said to have been painted in the 1700s. After the convent was discovered, the nuns were given 24 hours to leave the country; some went to the U.S., some to South America.

Jose next took them to a tile factory where souvenirs were custom-made for them, hand painted with figures, names, and dates. Marie bought a set of six mugs. Then to a leather shop making shoes and purses but no one bought anything there, then to a shop where tablecloths and napkins were being woven from maguey fiber. They all bought placemats just to have something made of that cactus fiber.

They were then taken to the Rosary Chapel (*Capilla del Rosario*) which, due to its splendor, has led it to be called the eighth wonder of the world. Construction was begun in 1571. Everyone agreed it was something out of this world. Gold leaf everywhere: ceilings, domes, sculptured figures, carvings. A statue of the Virgin Mary stood under the dome, enclosed in glass, said to be adorned with jewels and surrounded by floral bouquets of gold leaf. Jose told them that the adhesive holding the gold leaf consisted of bull's blood, lime, goat's milk, and egg whites. They were not encouraged to stay in the chapel as the girls were not dressed properly and were being stared at. They had been asked to cover their heads when they entered, but they were wearing slacks; Jose said that Mexicans believe that girls who wore slacks were no good. Eileen smoked and was told that Mexican women don't smoke except for very old ladies. Outside this ostentatious display of riches, blind men were begging for money.

Jose took them to Guadalupe Fort where the Battle of *Puebla* was fought on May 5 (*Cinco de Mayo*), 1862, located on a hill with a good view of the city. He said that nowadays this was where men came to settle their arguments. Coming down from the hill, they passed the governor's mansion and a very attractive home with a swimming pool and servants' quarters. Jose said the home was owned by a man who had once worked for his father, but he was a drunk and did such poor work he was fired. He got another job and, when he was paid for a day's work, instead of paying his bills he bought a lottery ticket, got a girl, and got drunk. The police hunted him for two days to tell him he had won five million pesos in the lottery. According to Jose, one could rent a nine-room house, furnished, with pool and servants' quarters for 500 pesos (US$100) a month.

Jose said he worked in his father's bakery but made 80 to 160 pesos a day by guiding tours. Some other trivia from Jose: All men must serve a year in the Army. At an intersection when driving, you must blow your horn twice, and the first one that blows has the right of way. City people arise at about 6:00 a.m., go home about 2:00 p.m. for siesta until 5:00 p.m., then go back to work until 8:00 or 9:00 p.m., go to bed between 11:00 and 12:00 p.m. They eat six courses at all three meals.

He took them to a grocery store to buy bread, then told them how to get out of town. They dropped him off near the police station and paid him 100 pesos. From an elevation of more than 7,000 ft. in *Puebla,* they descended to *Atlixco,* El. 3,300 ft., where they stopped to buy some fruit, eggs, and a dishpan, then departed to look for a place to stop for the night. After driving for an hour after dark, they found a place between I*zucar de Matamoras* and *Tehuitzingo* at about 5,000 ft., on a curve in the mountains. It was very warm. Persh almost backed off the mountain as he was turning around; he thought he was in first gear but was in reverse. The noise of an animal licking out an empty salmon can woke them up at 3:15 a.m. Persh thought it was a mountain lion and grabbed his gun, but it was only a dog. Later three burros appeared, just snooping around.

They woke up to find they had been bitten by gnats that left huge red marks around the bite. Persh cleaned the spark plugs of both vehicles before they left. Brown and yellow lizards more than a foot long darted here and there, and an iguana crossed the road in front of them. Saguaro and organ pipe cactus began to appear. They had now transitioned from mountainous back to tropical country. People lived in adobe and bamboo huts. Almost everyone went barefoot, and the children, even the boys, wore no pants. The car and truck attracted a lot of attention when they stopped for gas and a beer in *Acatlan.* Colorful rocks and stones bordered the roadway into *Chila,* after which the road climbed again as it crossed from the state of *Puebla* into the state of *Oaxaca.* The countryside here was quite desolate until after they left *Tamazulapan* where it became very scenic, resembling the Badlands of South Dakota with sand hills of green, red, orange, wine, white, and black, with wonderful views as they descended into *Yanhuitlan.* Cactus reappeared as they approached *Nochixtlan.* They observed people using a modern threshing machine, but the grain was being hauled away in oxcarts with wooden wheels. The girls took a picture of the foreman who apologized for not being dressed up. Here, and in many other places along the way, they had to stop and get the car wheels sprayed, and they themselves had to get out of the cars and walk through disinfectant as part of an effort to control hoof-and-mouth disease in livestock.

In *Nochixtlan* they stopped for a coke but had to drink it warm as ice was unavailable. In the Square, barefoot natives were waiting for the bus, some begging, some with chickens, and mothers feeding their babies who were wrapped and tied in shawls. Women were riding donkeys. It became apparent that people and animals were beginning to be shy and a little afraid of the travelers. South of town they saw pine trees again. They found a place to camp in an abandoned quarry away from the road a distance, very comfortable and cool with no bugs and no disturbances during the night.

Friday, April 30. They were startled awake at 7:00 a.m. by shots fired nearby, but the shots were followed by music from a band, then more shots which they deduced were from either a funeral or rehearsal for a *Cinco de Mayo* parade. The previous day they had heard gunshots at a funeral procession where a small casket covered with lovely flowers was being carried. People along the way were making tortillas, pounding them with rocks and baking them in ovens resembling domed bee hives (skeps). They hadn't traveled far before they discovered a flat on the right front tire of the truck and had to pull off the road to change it. When they resumed travel, the highway soon took them around the edge of a mountain and a wonderful panorama of the city of *Oaxaca* came into view.

Chapter 7: Oaxaca

Oaxaca was a much larger city than they expected. They were stopped again for disinfecting right at the city limits then, as luck would have it, spied a Chevrolet garage at the edge of town so they stopped and got the tire fixed. There was a convenient park across the street where modern records were being played in English. When they stopped at a downtown square for refreshments, they were immediately surrounded by men selling large, colorful wool rugs for 45 pesos. A boy ran up to Persh and told him in English he shouldn't pay that much. It turned out that the boy was sent by a man who introduced himself as Jesse Fulcher from Pecos, Texas. He

came over to say that there was a small town nearby where the rugs were made and he would take them there. Then another English-speaking fellow came over, a well-dressed Mexican who had spent some time in Oklahoma. Both men worked for the government "Hoof-and-Mouth Disease" project. The men told them where  to change money, get water, where to find a doctor for typhus and tetanus shots, directed them to the post office, Western Union, and then insisted on picking up the tab for their cokes and beers.

The doctor they found didn't speak English and they questioned his competence, but he apparently knew what he was doing although the needle he used was very dull. After lunch, they went to the Hotel Monte Alban to get some pure drinking water. The hotel had none but sent a cute little boy with them to find water. Jesse, the Texan, went along. The boy took them down some terrible streets that were all dug up because the city was putting in a new sewer system. The original sewer, which had been put in many years before by a German ship captain, had collapsed. The first place they went had no water, but the boy knew another place that had pure water: 10 gallons for 50¢.

Jesse called his driver, Manuel, and escorted the travelers to a tiny Indian village about 15 miles outside town where colorful serapes and rugs were made. The streets seemed deserted until they stopped in an alley. Then people poured out of nowhere with their rugs, bartering and urging them to buy, but their asking prices were 90-150 pesos which seemed too much. And although Jesse and Manuel, who spoke Spanish, urged the vendors to lower their prices, no one bought anything. An old man came to the car, pointed at the aerial, and motioned as if turning a dial. Marie turned the radio on and soon the car was surrounded by people of all sizes and ages mesmerized by the music and voices coming from thin air.

On the way back to town, they stopped at a churchyard in the town of *El Tule* to see a very old tree[8], said to be 2-3,000 years old. They were told it was a cypress but Eileen believed it to be a pine of some kind and described it as being so huge it was unbelievable, that words could not describe it: 160 ft. around the base and 168 ft. high.

It was dark when they got back to the city which was very much alive. Zapotec and Mixtec Indians were predominate here. A debate was held on whether to leave town, but the decision was made to stay after Jesse and his friend told them that May 1 and May 5 were not good days for Americans to be on the road because those days are holidays, people who don't like gringos get drunk, and the roads south were being repaired by work gangs from northern Mexico who had a reputation for being extra tough customers. While sitting in the cars trying to decide, the blanket men mobbed them so they could hardly open the car doors. Babe, Jan and Pic each bought a rug; Babe's was the prettiest and she paid US$7 for it. They checked into the *Marquis de Valles* Hotel on the square, got three rooms for two nights for 4½ pesos per person, rushed to change clothes and enjoyed a fabulous five-course meal at the hotel. After dinner, they returned to their rooms, sat at their windows and watched the people in the park and on the street below. A marimba band passed under their windows followed by a crowd drinking tequila. The band played until 12:45 a.m. When they quit, the birds in the park continued singing just as if it were daylight.

<u>Saturday, May 1.</u> Labor Day, a federal public holiday, was celebrated with parades, rallies, large crowds, and public speakers promoting workers' rights. The day started off at 6:30 a.m. with everything that could make a noise doing so: bells, horns, chimes, drums, whistles. At 9 a.m. a single band went by, at 11 a.m. a band and a group of civilians passed, at 12:30 p.m. two bands and a mob of people went by and stopped on the square. Two men gave speeches, one accusing the gringos of taking their land away from them. The people going by were carrying everything imaginable on their heads to market: cement blocks, baskets, long trays of rolls, etc. After a satisfying lunch in the dining room, the group decided they would go to the market. It was a filthy, hot, crowded mess but, even so, proved to be very interesting. There was everything in the way of strange fruit, but for them the worst part was the meat markets with the meat out in the open and flies crawling all over it. They bought a few items: a sombrero ashtray, a knife, some

pottery. After a beer on the square, they met Jesse back at the hotel and decided, even though it was nearly dark, to drive out to the pre-Columbian archaeological ruins of Monte Alban[9]. A winding gravel road took them to the top of a hill about six miles west of town. Over the centuries, the ruins had been covered by earth. Excavation had not begun until 1939 so only a portion had been uncovered by 1948. They walked up a hill to the temple where a guide, for a fee, took them to a locked tomb and gave a lecture, most of which they didn't understand. The tomb was 4x8 ft.; above the door were stone idols with faces and lions, and on each side of the tomb were insets in the stone with pots containing emeralds and other precious jewels; there were also signs of spoiled food. There were dim paintings on the walls, and outside there were paintings and carvings on stone slabs, each about 3x5 ft. The designs presumably had significance to the ancients but not to the tourists.

On the road back down, they marveled at the beauty of the lights of the city below them. After a good dinner at the hotel, Babe, Pic, and Eileen went with Jesse out on the streets and bartered for blankets. Babe bought two very attractive large ones and two smaller ones. Throughout the trip, she shopped for items that she could sell when she returned to Wisconsin. Then everyone returned to the hotel for a good night's sleep.

Chapter 8: Getting To Guatemala

Sunday, May 2. Jesse woke them at 6:30 a.m. and joined them for breakfast, after which they packed up, paid their bill, and left at noon. He led them to a gas station where they were limited to 20 liters (5.3 gallons) so they had to drive back into town to fuel up both vehicles. No sooner had they passed from flatland to colorful mountains than they encountered the road construction Jesse had told them about: rocks on the road, left, right, piles of rocks everywhere. When they finally passed through the mountains, they found themselves in a tropical area again. There were lots of parrots in the trees, mostly in pairs, and a few villages where the natives were enjoying Sunday by resting and swimming in the nude. Near a bridge under construction they came upon a small food stand where they were able to get beer, cokes, and fruit. The stand had piles of locally grown coconuts, 40¢ each, so they bought a couple. Shortly before entering *Tehuantepec,* they had to stop at a disinfectant station where the gravel road gave way to a very welcome tar road. A mile or two beyond this there was a bridge under construction and they found themselves on a detour on which it was necessary to ford the *Tehuantepec* River; fortunately it was quite shallow. Here they first heard the very disturbing news that the highway south to Guatemala was under construction and closed to through traffic. It became apparent that their only option would be to ship the cars by rail to the Guatemalan border.

Tehuantepec[10] struck them as being a dirty town but it was Sunday and everyone was all dressed up, eating in the park. There were pretty girls with very colorful skirts and blouses made of handkerchiefs. They found a very nice spot off the road near a stream in "Texas-like" country to camp for the night. Jesse and Manuel had followed them from *Oaxaca* and joined them for dinner. Manuel gave them two coconuts when he left. The cars were parked just off an ox road where carts of bananas and coconuts rumbled by all night. Jesse told them the produce was hauled at night in

28

order to avoid the extreme heat of the daytime.

Ants were crawling all over dirty dishes the next morning so Pic and Marie washed the dishes in the creek before they ate breakfast. Since there was no rail service in *Tehuantepec*, they had to drive to the nearest station which was in *Ixetepec*, a small town twenty miles north. Jesse had arranged to meet them there at the local headquarters for the Hoof-and-Mouth Commission for which he worked. There they met Dr. Wilson, a very pleasant man in charge, who prescribed some anti-malarial tablets for them. He spoke no English but had an interpreter, Rafael Banana, a Chilean who had studied at the University of California and had surprisingly married a girl from Kansas City. They all went to the railroad station to find out about shipping the cars. There was a train leaving that afternoon but the charge was 448 pesos (US$90) for a box-car plus having to pay for help to load and unload the cars, plus passenger fares. After a group discussion, the decision was made to drive on to *Arriaga* and catch the train there as it was 123 miles closer to the border.

They left *Ixetepec* after getting gas and air and some cokes. The countryside was very flat, dry, and dusty for miles. As the terrain became more mountainous they caught their first glimpse of the Pacific Ocean. Another tire went flat, the right back on the truck. A flock of parrots and some pink spoonbills entertained them while the tire was being changed. One of the coconuts was cracked and eaten. A stopping place was found in the mountains where the car radio played the Lux Theatre and music from the States during dinner. A cool night's sleep was enjoyed by all.

Tuesday, May 4. A gloriously beautiful sunrise greeted them when they awoke at 5:30. Eileen felt sick to her stomach, and riding along on a rough gravel road didn't help. They took a wrong road and headed to *Las Cruces* but were corrected by some villagers and were relieved to find a decent paved road when they rejoined the highway. They were served warm drinks at a roadside stand by a jolly woman who wanted to learn English. The paved road soon gave way to a very narrow winding gravel road that took them down into *Arriaga* where it was steaming hot. When they stopped for drinks and inquired about the roads, they met a fellow from Illinois who told them there was a road *"so to speak"* to *Tonala*, about fifteen miles down the road, so they gassed up and decided to chance it. The one-lane road seemed defiant, daring them to pass through. It was very bumpy, through jungle and dry creek beds. Persh discovered he was covered with tiny ticks that he got while roaming around in the woods. When they came to a pleasant creek where people and cattle were bathing, he plunged in and took a bath with the natives while the girls dangled their feet in the cool water.

They arrived in *Tonala* at 5:00 p.m. and were immediately met by a man from the station who gave them information about shipping the cars. They were told that the women had to go by passenger train leaving at 11:00 a.m. the next morning, arriving at the border station at 7:00 p.m. on that day. Persh would go with the cars, leaving at 4:00 a.m. There were two hotels in town, both miserable, but before they checked into one Persh showed up with written permission for all of them to ride on the platform with the cars, so they proceeded to load the cars in the dark. Right off the bat the rear of the truck caught on the incline as the spare tire hung down too low, and in no time at all the whole town turned out to watch the show. Some pitched in to help including a drunk guy who really tried their patience. Another man, trying to use the big car jack, bent the rear bumper and chipped the paint on one of the doors. Their help was worse than no help at all. Persh got very angry at them but tried to conceal it to maintain good-will with the crowd. As a last resort, he decided to use the block and tackle, their first experience in using it. Pic and Jan pitched in and got some of the townspeople to help as well. Pic entertained a group of boys with her efforts but Jan stole the show to the amusement of the crowd because of her yelling, pulling, and working right up there on the flatcar with the men. Eventually Persh handed Eileen the end of the rope and told her to hold on tight and start walking with it which she did for a great distance followed by a large crowd. Finally, on looking back she saw the truck was safely aboard the platform. The car went aboard very handily, and they all relaxed and ate cheese and crackers except Persh who supervised tying the cars down. Some of the crowd stayed to listen to the car radio.

They spent the night in the loaded cars without much sleep as a marimba band played until after midnight and the workers started making up the 4:00 a.m. train at 2:45. A man came to inform them that they didn't have the proper papers but he could get them for a small fee and their flatcar would get connected to the 6:00 a.m. train. They were  charged 190 pesos for the flatcar, 80 pesos for six first-class tickets, 5 pesos for the switchman, 20 pesos for the ticket man, and 45 pesos for various loading charges for a total of 340 pesos (US$68). They considered these charges exorbitant but paid them since there was no alternative. Their flatcar was switched up and down, moved here and there, and finally left the station at 10:40 a.m. The heat had been nearly unbearable so it was a relief to get moving and feel a breeze. At first they rode right on the flatcar, but it was so dusty and dirty that they sought relief in the cars. There they nearly got seasick from rocking and rolling on the bumpy old track. When the ticket collector came, he invited them to sit in the caboose which was neat and clean, though old and rickety. They were treated well, provided with beds and pillows and limes to quench their thirst. Jan became quite sick with a temperature of 104°. She had diarrhea and, as a result of a mostly liquid diet, they all had to pee badly but there were no bathroom facilities except at the few stops the train made. At one stop Persh bought a large loaf of bread, so they dined on Spam sandwiches with pickles, tomatoes, and mayonnaise; a meal that Marie described as *really good*. The scenery was tropical: banana and coconut plantations, rubber trees, sapotes, elephant ears, wildflowers. People were friendly: women washing clothes, dishes, themselves, their hair, in the same water with cows and pigs and nude bathers. Mosquitos became a nuisance so they took Aralen (chloroquine) pills that Dr. Wilson had prescribed for

31

malaria. Their destination was *Tapachula*, very near the Guatemalan border, the center of a major agricultural area that specialized in coffee.

They arrived in *Tapachula* at 9:00 p.m. and were greeted by two boys who wanted to unload the cars for a fee. Instead, the boys settled for escorting Pic and Jan to the International Hotel to get a room for Jan to rest. The hotel room left much to be desired; no hot water, the telephone didn't work, they got all the noise from the street, and the shower was in the middle of the bathroom. But Jan felt better the next day; she was very weak but the fever had subsided. The others stayed on the flatcar to spend another night made nearly sleepless by being bumped around as the flatcar was relocated from place to place. It ended up between boxcars and an engine that was getting up steam at 4:00 a.m. and persisted in blowing its steam onto their flatcar.

The next morning, a man from Los Angeles approached them to tell of conditions in Guatemala: *"bad roads and raining like hell"*. He said he had been driving south with four men, their back wheel hit a rock which threw them onto a soft shoulder and down an embankment. They escaped with only minor scratches, but he was abandoning his car and heading back north. He said he'd had to get a permit to unload his car before 11:00 a.m. or it would be charged and not released for another day, so Persh rushed 13 blocks to find the permit office. They tried to stall him there, but he was able to get the permit issued in time. While he was gone, Eileen and Babe met Happy Lonya, an American fruit buyer from Utica, New York, who bought them a beer and gave them some tips and addresses. When Persh returned, he got involved with the railroad people who wanted an extra 400 pesos because of the heavy load. Happy interpreted and haggled to get the price down to 206 pesos. Then the railroad wanted 35 pesos to untie the ropes that held the cars, but Persh wanted to do it himself. Happy made them understand "NO", but they charged 35 pesos for setting up each plank which Persh paid very begrudgingly. When the cars were finally freed, Marie, Persh, and Eileen untangled 408 feet of rope, a very hot and dirty job that left them black with dirt or, as Marie put it *"blacker than we already were from the train ride*". Not until they got to Guatemala did they realize they had left the block-and-tackle at the railroad station.

Everybody went to the Hotel Internacional where Happy treated them all to beer and big pitchers of lemonade which really hit the spot. They all washed and showered in Pic and Jan's room, then had lunch, followed by a visit to the Guatemalan consul and a trip to the beach which was about 15 miles out of town. The beach had black sand and was fairly clean. They swam until early evening even though the waves were very large and there was a strong undertow. Happy had ridden to the beach with them, so the girls took him back to town and checked out of the hotel while the others set up camp in the beach parking lot. They had dinner when the girls returned at 10:30 p.m. and were pestered by mosquitos all night. They couldn't find their sheets so they covered themselves with wool blankets despite the heat. Marie said she couldn't leave even a big toe uncovered or the mosquitos would bite it in a dozen places. Next morning they were awakened early by swimmers and by *chachalucas*, noisy birds that made loud clucking and chattering sounds. Marie and Eileen sunbathed until the others got up, then all performed housecleaning on the vehicles. Most of the day was spent sleeping. Persh fished and caught gaftops (sail catfish) and whiting which he cleaned for a fish fry for dinner. That night they sprayed the cars for mosquitos, slept with the windows up, found some sheets, and had a much better night's sleep

Saturday, May 8. Marie's 25th birthday. A group of local fellows came by to take them fishing. They drove five or six miles down a bumpy road to a hut and parked. From there, some walked and some took a boat made from a hollowed-out log to a pleasant point where the ocean washed into a picturesque bay, very calm and perfect for swimming. The group caught eight gaftops before the ocean became really rough. Marie scared them all by venturing out too far in the water to fish. She caught three fish but was upset that in the undertow she lost her special "University of Wisconsin" towel. Persh hooked a 50-lb. shark that fought him for a long time and eventually chewed the line in two and swam away.

33

Everybody went in for a final dip. As they drove away from the ocean breeze, they discovered that everyone was sunburned except Marie. Jan was very badly burned, so they ran for Unguentine and any kind of oil or ointment that might help. Back at camp they had an early dinner, fished until dark, and retired early as there was nothing else to do.

Sunday, May 9. Having had enough sun, surf, sand, mosquitos, and heat, they packed up and drove back to *Tapachula*. When they went to Mexican customs, a very agreeable English-speaking man in charge asked what was in the truck and wanted to see the car titles. He said the roads to Guatemala were very bad; also, once across the border, everything would have to be removed from the vehicles and required to be fumigated for four hours. They all adjourned to the hotel to learn there was no lemonade so had to settle for cokes and beer. People were passing in and out and celebrating as it was Election Day. Happy came in and invited everyone to visit a barbecue that *Señor Palomeque*, who owned the hotel and was running for office, was sponsoring to get votes. Seven cows had been barbecued in huge pits in which fires were built to heat bricks. The cows were wrapped in palm leaves, put in the pits, covered with dirt and cooked overnight. Country people were brought in by trucks, entertained and fed, to get their votes. The meat looked delicious. Then it was announced that *Palomeque* had won his race, so the celebration drew to a close and everybody left.

When they returned to the hotel, Pic and Jan had discovered that they had lost a billfold which they last remembered having there at the hotel. It contained $200 in traveler's checks and U.S. dollars plus the title to the truck. A search of the hotel and inquiry at the desk came up empty as did a return to the barbecue place. Pic and Babe saw the customs agent who took them to the local radio station where an announcement was broadcast every half hour for five hours. Pic and Jan stayed in their room while the rest went out to eat. While they were eating, a cute little boy brought the billfold to the girls. Someone had slipped it onto the billiard table and nothing was missing except $8.

A large crowd assembled on the street and a band started to play as the newly elected Governor of the state of *Chiapas, Francisco Grajales,* had arrived and was out on the balcony making a speech. Happy Lanyo, whose real first name was Mariano, came from just having met the Governor at the airport and invited the group to dinner. He paid for a very good meal of soup and steak at the hotel. During dinner he entertained them by telling stories of things he had experienced in his travels and younger days. Then they all went to the park to watch the people. As the band played, boys walked one direction and girls the other until they found someone they liked, then they walked together as a couple. Happy talked the travelers out of heading for the border and camping out yet that night because of bandits on the road, so they slept in the cars at the hotel; Marie in the truck, Persh and Eileen in the car. Babe was with Pic and Jan in their hotel room. Persh said Eileen snored so hard that the car rocked.

Chapter 9: Guatemala

<u>Monday, May 10.</u> Happy woke them up at 7:30 a.m. After a very fine breakfast at the hotel, they left for the border. At a station just outside town, they were stopped and asked a few questions; from there it was nine miles to the crossover point at Talisman Bridge. As they approached the bridge, they had to stop at the Mexican border station where they were asked about purchases in Mexico; the record of a truck tire they had purchased had an error that needed to be corrected. A deposit of 59 pesos was required, to be refunded on their return to Mexico, but they argued that they were not returning so the fee was waived. The inspectors noticed that Pic's ankles were swollen from sunburn and suggested that Guatemalan inspectors probably wouldn't let her in for fear of Hoof-and-Mouth disease, so Pic put on bedroom slippers, socks, and pants that would cover her legs. Truck mileage at the border was 6,184.

Once the bridge was crossed into Guatemala, they drove through disinfectant, then had to get out and walk through disinfectant, then the wheels were sprayed after which they had a confrontation with the chief officer. He instructed them to remove everything from the truck to a shed where it would be fumigated. Marie asked whether they could transfer everything into the truck, close it up, and fumigate it. Surprisingly, the officials agreed. Fumigation took four hours, from 11:00 a.m. to 3:00 p.m. The time was spent with refreshments, clearing their passports, and changing money into quetzals, the Guatemalan currency which were worth one dollar each. After that they went down to the *Suchiate*, a very pleasant river that ran under the bridge, and sat on rocks to cool their swollen feet in the water. A burro was tied to a bush beside them; upstream, people were swimming and washing. Pigs, chickens, ducks, dogs, and goats wandered about.

Once the truck was released, they were relieved to be on their way. They soon came to a fellow directing traffic at a turn in the road. Persh asked which way to Guatemala City and was directed to the right where they almost immediately came to a dead-end where stood a customs inspection station. The girls were marched into a large building. Everything in the car had to be pulled out and placed on a bench where all items were listed, then put back in the car. The truck was next. Bystanders and inspectors stood around with their mouths agape, amazed at all the things that were hauled out. Gifts of cigarettes and crackers were of some help in breaking the ice (Persh gave the chief a carton of Camels) but, as a whole, the work crew impressed the group as being a very sour, homely, and dirty lot with no sense of humor. The travelers gritted their teeth, smiled and acted nonchalant to mask their indignation over the heavy-handedness of the inspection. One thing the inspectors missed was Persh's pistol for which he did not have a permit; not for lack of trying, however, as he had wired for permission in Mexico City and applied again in *Tapachula* but was told to get it in Guatemala City. The inspectors even pawed through their canned food but did not confiscate any of it, so the hungry bunch ate beans, graham crackers, and peanut butter while waiting. At 6:15 p.m. the officials called a halt to the process as the office officially closed at 6:00 p.m., so things were rapidly stowed away, fortunately, because the inspectors had not gotten into all their compartments yet. The journey continued just as it was getting dark and a torrential rain commenced.

Visibility was near zero. The road forward was very narrow, nearly covered with water, and took them over a rickety old bridge that they feared might collapse. To their relief they made it into *Malacatan* and stopped for a beer at a hotel where they encountered a character who transported cars into Guatemala. He struck them as being rather shady as he tried so hard to be helpful, too helpful in their opinion. He had a friend who had bought beer for Babe and Marie at the border and had that certain look in his eye. They were told they could rent a room with dinner and breakfast for $2 each, but the rooms had no doors! Marie seemed to be the only one who suspected that this hotel was, or had been, a brothel and convinced the others that they should leave. Their suspicions became really aroused when the two characters insisted on showing them to the highway. Persh armed himself with his revolver and the caravan took off. They were led out into the country and at a certain point were told to turn left two kilometers ahead, but they turned right to thwart the guides. Just across a bridge, they found a suitable place to stop. They all ate in the car and talked for quite a while. Persh and Pic told stories about some of the things they did when they were kids. Babe and Marie slept in the backseat of the car, Pic and Jan in front, Persh and Eileen in the truck. They hadn't been asleep long before those in the truck were awakened by a flashlight in their eyes and a face at the window. The adrenaline rushed as they feared it was the two men from the hotel, but a man's voice mumbled something to which Persh loudly replied *"no problemo"*. He believed the man was drunk or crazy, stumbling, jabbering, and shining his light around. Soon the headlights on the car flashed, the horn honked, and Persh ran back to find that the man was trying to get into the car, testing all the doors and vents. The girls laid still and covered their faces. After all that, they decided to go back on the highway where they found themselves climbing uphill on a very bad narrow road, half mud, half stone, and nearly washed out. They were soon stymied by a small hill that was so deep in mud that it was impassable, so they backed down the road a ways and slept in the cars right in the middle of the roadway until daylight.

Tuesday, May 11. They were awakened at 6:10 a.m. by a truckload of men behind them, unable to get around. Those men pushed all the vehicles up the hill by hand, first the panel truck, then the car, then their own truck. Once over the hill, the road turned to cobblestone but climbed and climbed with very sharp narrow curves as the road ascended 7,000 ft. in the next 40 miles up into the cool highlands. The roadside was very tropical and quite heavily populated. They bought some eggs and found a place to stop and fix breakfast. Gas at a Shell station in *San Marcos* was 58¢ per gallon which was considered exorbitant since gas back in the States was only 20¢. None of them had any local money and the station wouldn't accept traveler's checks, but a fellow who spoke English helped them out by swapping some dollars for quetzals. Leaving San Marcos, the road became wider and somewhat improved but extremely bumpy. The rack holding the spare tire was jarred off the truck and had to be stowed inside. From there to Guatemala City, the road wound through the most densely populated area of the country, up mountain passes to highlands, down into warm valleys, through ancient Indian villages, never losing sight of a stately row of volcanoes. The Guatemalan Congress had designated this road the "Franklin D. Roosevelt Highway".

Queztaltenango was a very lovely town. Spring flowers were abundant: calla lilies, roses, sweet peas, geraniums----also magnolia and coffee trees. While the rest of the crew went to the market, Eileen stayed in the truck with a swollen ankle and collected quite an audience. The group at the market was bombarded by men selling handsome Guatemalan-designed soft wool blankets which were priced $12-$28. Nobody bought a large one but Marie and Babe each bought a small piece for $1.25. Marie's purchase measured 30x32 inches and depicted two native men, one playing a reed instrument, the other banging a  drum, with a border legend reading *"Hecho En Guatemala"*. Women gawked and giggled at Jan's shorts. A native fellow was fascinated by Pic and followed her around. After they left town, the road improved significantly, still gravel and bumpy but wide. As they drove from one town to the other they saw natives heading to the nearest market carrying all kinds of things on their backs and heads. At one spot, they stopped for what appeared to be a rock in the road but as they walked near it they discovered it was being dynamited so they rushed back, reaching the safety of their cars just as it blew up. Gas stations with familiar names, Esso, Texaco, Shell, became more common. The countryside here was quite flat with farmland and the *Atitlan* volcano looming in the distant background. They bought homegrown produce along the way for a wonderful early dinner of steak, potatoes, peas and carrots for a total cost of about US$1.85, then found a grand camping spot back from the road, shaded by trees, sheltered by a cliff.

Some native families visited during breakfast the next morning. Babe gave a little girl a piece of jewelry; a red pin. Persh repaired the spare tire rack, re-mounted it, and checked the oil in both cars. Before they had gone very far, the road crossed a creek where a man in a truck was stuck. All got out, rolled up their pant legs and helped push him out; then Marie, Jan, and Eileen pushed their truck through. In so doing, Eileen fell in the mud and later discovered her watch was missing. She went back, dug and scratched in the mud, finally found the watch intact and still running.

Totonicapan, the next town, was quite attractive. When they stopped for cigarettes, kids swarmed all over them, kids that Eileen described as *"very dirty with blank expressions and homely looks on their faces, horribly big teeth and all with colds. And ditto for the adults who commonly exhibited a sour disposition, although city folks weren't quite as bad as in the smaller places"*. As soon as they left *Totonicapan,* the road became worse as it began a very steep climb with sharp hairpin curves. The radiators started to boil even though the gauges registered only 170°F. The scenery became striking with pine trees scenting the air. Climbing continued into strange-looking country, very desolate with scattered rocks and a few shacks here and there for sheepherders who tended the many fine-looking black sheep grazing there. The road took them across the top of *Los Encuentros* to an elevation of 11,000 ft., after which it slowly descended into *Sololá* perched atop a cliff overlooking Lake Atitlan[11] *(Lago Atitlan)*. A roadway of constantly winding curves descended 2,000 ft. to *Panajachel,* a quaint village on the north shore of the lake. Gorgeous flowers were everywhere; Marie said they were *"the most beautiful flowers she had ever seen"*. There were cars full of Americans driving around--- some had chauffeurs. Their caravan wandered by mistake into a very nice hotel right on the lake where a retired U.S. Army veteran came out to talk, told them the names of the flowers and the best place to camp. There were two brightly colored macaws on the lawn; one flew right at them and landed on a nearby fence. To get to the campsite, they drove down a steep embankment to a wonderful parking area on a perfect beach with a view of five volcanoes. There was an Indian herding cows there. When Marie asked him if it was all right for them to camp there, he replied *"como no"* ("of course"). Fishing was unsuccessful but a trip to town provided three chickens for 85¢, enough for two meals.

<u>Thursday, May 13</u>. Marie woke up early and saw fish jumping all over the lake, but the fishing gear was with Persh who was fast asleep. When he finally got up he went fishing with a small Guatemalan man, but they caught only one tiny fish. The little native stayed for breakfast and visited with them all morning. Marie did laundry in the lake. They left the campground at 10:30 a.m. and decided to go to *Antigua*, about ten miles off the highway. It was a larger city than they expected. *Antigua* (meaning  Old) was once the colonial capital of the Spanish Kingdom of Guatemala. It has been persistently damaged by earthquakes over several centuries due to its proximity to the three volcanoes towering more than 13,000 ft. nearby: *Fuego, Agua,* and *Acatenango. Fuego* was still smoking from a recent eruption. The travelers met steady streams of people with ox carts and huge loads of baskets. Persh tried to take movies of some women washing at a fountain and they all ran off. There was a large market with a good selection of fruit and vegetables. Inside the market they met Bernardino, a young boy who spoke English and offered to be their guide. He promised their first stop would be a surprise, a visit to a home called *Casa de las Campanas,* a popular tourist stop. Their knock on the door was answered by Mildred Covill Palmer, a very tall, attractive American woman with white hair. Mrs. Palmer had a shop of Guatemalan articles and welcomed them to look through her more than 300-year-old home. Everything was spotless, each room opening to the patio which was occupied by two brilliantly colored macaws. Mrs. Palmer, one of only a dozen Americans living in *Antigua*, had lived in Guatemala for 20 years and was well known there for her restaurant in Guatemala City and for advocating the artistry of Guatemalan weaving. She designed her own

clothes, had her own carpenter and had designed everything in the house, furniture and all. Each room had a tiny cedar-filled fireplace in some surprising spot. Marie's description: "*It was really exquisite, just like a dream, everything modern as could be, done in the best of taste and so very original*" Bernardino next took them to the Monastery[12] which struck them as a bunch of ruins. Then to San Franciscan church[13], another ruin. Next stop was at a silver shop in a hotel where a cute little girl named Conchita brought a basket of her jewelry to a table. She captivated everyone with her personality and originality. Eileen couldn't resist buying a wedding chain and ring for $13. Conchita had a mock marriage performed with Eileen and Persh by looping the chain over both their necks, a priest conducted a short ceremony, then Persh looped the chain over Eileen again, put the ring on her finger and kissed her. It was customary to give the priest thirteen coins. By this time it was getting late. They gave Bernardino 75¢ and left town only to discover ten miles later that they were going the wrong direction, so they retraced their steps back to the highway where they found an unfinished section of road on which to camp for the night.

Friday, May 14. A breathtaking sight greeted them the next morning: the sunlit, snow-capped tops of the three volcanoes rising out of a dense fog. After breakfast, they headed for Guatemala City about twenty miles away. Six miles out, the road provided a good view of the city below and slowly descended down into it. They checked into the Pan American Hotel, a very pleasant place with a charming lobby and dining room, striking tile floors, palms, vines and flowers all around, and two doormen dressed in colorful outfits. Rooms were $13 with meals provided. Marie shared a room with Babe and lingered in it as long as she could as "*it was such a lovely room I wanted to enjoy it as much as possible*". It reminded her of the room she had occupied in the Excelsior Hotel in Rome. The day was spent doing laundry, shopping, and sight-seeing. A highlight event was finding ice cream and sodas in a modern drugstore filled with American products. In the hotel lobby, they ran into Ted Southworth, a young man from Springfield, Massachusetts who had just graduated from Dartmouth. He was a short story writer and also wrote articles for his hometown newspaper. He was headed for Santiago too but was hitch-hiking. He carried a small satchel and a sleeping bag and slept on the ground. He said he drank the local water and ate native food but had no shots, not even for malaria. He was going to climb one of the active volcanos the next day. That evening they went to Ciro's, a modern night club with a good orchestra and 50¢ beer.

After breakfast the next morning they went to the coffee factory, headquarters for Guatemalan coffee from which one-million 150-lb. barrels of coffee beans were being shipped to the U.S. every year. The visitors were served coffee, taken on a quick tour, and given a one-pound bag of pure Guatemalan coffee. The price of coffee in the stores was 35¢/lb. Then a quick stop to *"a dirty old market said to be the worst in Guatemala"* where they looked for bargains and bought some pottery at a very cheap price. Checkout time at the hotel was noon, so they hurried back to pack. They had brought in so much luggage that it required several trips to the cars. On the first trip, the manager thought they were trying to skip out without paying and became very upset. Before hitting the road, they made a stop at a filling station, a trip to the drugstore for final shots (another dull needle), and a search for potable water which ended with them getting tap water from the swanky Hotel Victoria. There were so many roads out of town they had to ask for directions several times, so when they left the city it was already time to find a place to camp for the night. They finally found a pleasant green spot bordering a flowing creek that served as a popular watering place for horses, cows, and people. Mileage when they left Guatemala City was 6,450.

The next morning everyone made good use of the creek. Persh cleaned the car's carburetor and they were on the road by 12:30 p.m. They were descending now from 4,500 ft. at Guatemala City to 2,900 ft. at *Jalapa* where they passed over a river, the *Rio Los Esclavos*, on a stone bridge constructed in 1592. They encountered one bad muddy spot on a detour which the car barely navigated without getting stuck. The country changed rapidly from tropical to pines to cactus. There were many birds, lots of parrots, and some delightful birds having a very narrow long tail, feathered at the end, which they later learned was the national bird of El Salvador, a turquoise-browed motmot, locally called a *torogoz*. Near the border they spied a lake where they wanted to camp but couldn't find an entrance. A young boy showed them a rocky little road but they had to cross a plowed field to get to the lake. Since the skies looked stormy, they camped right on the pathway. It was a peaceful, quiet, isolated spot and everybody slept very well. The moon was so bright they didn't need any other light. At the border next day, they learned that the lake was full of crocodiles.

Chapter 10: El Salvador

<u>Monday, May 17.</u> They awoke to face the ordeal of crossing the border into El Salvador. Thanks to an English-speaking guard it took only about fifteen minutes to get through Guatemalan customs. Seven miles later El Salvadoran customs inspection took 45 minutes as the inspectors wanted some paperwork, took baggage out and opened it, but they didn't really examine anything closely. The head inspector fell for Babe, gave her flowers, wanted a picture of her and was thrilled to receive a copy of her passport photo. Eileen entertained the work crew with maps of the States and maps showing the route they had traveled to get to El Salvador. She thought the Salvadoran people were *"better looking and showed more sense than Guatemalans"*. In *Santa Ana*, El Salvador's second largest city and a major coffee center, they changed dollars into colons (2½ colons per dollar), visited the market, and found a good drugstore, but when they asked for chocolate sodas they got giggles and chocolate ice cream. Prices in the market seemed a little higher than in Guatemala but were still very cheap. In a huge meat market, they saw pigs being butchered and bought 3 lbs. of fresh liver for a dollar.

After leaving *Santa Ana,* they asked for directions to *Lake Coatepeque* which was only a few miles off the highway to look for a place to camp. The road dropped down a steep mountain to the lake and village. It was a beautiful little mountain lake, but the village was so densely populated and commercialized that they had given up hope of finding a place to camp when they strayed onto a private road that led to the Hotel Monterrey where they were welcomed by Rema, a very large Great Dane. Soon Herbert Allisat, the hotel manager, and his mother came out to talk. Herbert spoke English and claimed an interesting background. He said he was a German lawyer who had gone to Washington, D.C. in 1938 to defend a German painter. When he returned to Germany, he was arrested for being anti-Nazi. Upon his release, he and his mother escaped through

Switzerland, found passage on a boat to Panama, and eventually settled in El Salvador. As a German national, he had some narrow escapes. When the U. S. entered the war, he was placed under house arrest for a year, then taken to the U.S. and spent some time in an internment camp (he called it a "concentration") camp and also worked in harvest and oil fields. When the war ended, he said he was detained on Ellis Island for six months, then given thirty days to leave the country, ending up back in El Salvador and finding this job as hotel manager. The group made a deal with him that they would eat their meals at his hotel but sleep and live in the cars and he would refrigerate their liver. After a delicious dinner, Marie asked Herbert about the government of El Salvador. He said they had what they called a democracy. The President is elected for four years, but he is usually an Army General who is supported by loyal troops who create riots and cause troubles to intimidate people into voting for them.

They intended to leave the next morning but after a huge breakfast at the hotel they swam in the lake, rented a boat and fished but caught only a couple of small wapotis, a very cute tropical fish. They decided to stay another night and spent the next day relaxing, writing letters, reading, and swimming. The water was perfect for swimming, clean, and just the right temperature. Persh took a one-man raft out into the middle of the lake to fish for 3½ hours but caught nothing. After dinner, Herbert and his mother joined them and they talked until bedtime.

Wednesday, May 19. After a very pleasant farewell breakfast with Herbert, they paid their bill and said their good-byes only to discover that the battery in the truck was dead----someone had left the ignition switch on. The hill was too steep for the car to pull the truck so they switched batteries and the truck pulled the car until it started. The road into the capital city, San Salvador, was excellent as were all the roads in El Salvador. They picked up Ted Southworth when they found him on the road just as they came into the city. After visits to the markets and shops, they concluded that San Salvador was a very disappointing town for a capital city. They made their important stops at the Embassy and the Honduran and Nicaraguan consuls for visas, then split up, with the girls going to get groceries and water. Persh and Eileen went back to the market, then spent 2½ hours looking for the girls, finally finding them at a brewery. They were there not to drink beer but to get some pure water. Gas was 48¢/gallon: *Embajadores* cigarettes, 35¢ a pack. It started to rain just as they left town. They were soon in an area where the cars were a novelty. Ox carts with wooden wheels were common as were people washing and bathing in creeks. They kept driving until they crossed the *Lempa* River on the 1,350 ft. *Cuscatlan* Bridge, the longest suspension bridge in Central America and a gift to El Salvador from the U.S. They pulled in to eat at a truck stop that had a food stand and decided to sit up all night there in the cars as it was still raining hard.

The bridge traffic woke them up next morning. Everything was green from the rain as they drove through nice-looking hill country to *San Miguel.* At a drugstore to buy more Aralen, they encountered a fellow who had studied in California and showed them an article in a California magazine about three men who had terminated their trip to Costa Rica because the road was too bad. The man recommended consulting a Mr. Griffin at the nearby Port of *La Union* who might be knowledgeable and helpful as, if this were the case, it appeared the cars would need to be shipped by boat. At the port, Mr. Griffin told them they should be able to drive to *Managua* with no difficulty; he provided a name and address in *Managua* where more information would be available. From *La Union,* the border was 21 miles away over deteriorating roads through a very dry countryside.

Chapter 11: Honduras

<u>Thursday, May 20.</u> They reached the Honduras border at 1:30 p.m. and learned that it didn't open until 2:00, but once it opened it took only twenty minutes to clear. Everyone was congenial with no troubles encountered. Truck mileage was 6,812. The road took them through country flat as Texas with numerous places suitable for camping, but the girls wanted to drive on. When they came to a customs spot, they were asked whether their trip was political or diplomatic. All at once they heard loud cries of "On Wisconsin" and "Hey, Indiana" and were surrounded by four American soldiers who were stationed in a camp nearby. The men were in Honduras to show the locals how to use new road equipment shipped from the States and to aid in military training for Honduran troops. They seemed overjoyed to see some fellow Americans. Smokey was from Baltimore, Herb from Indiana, Ben from Texas, and Ed from Spain. Smokey was the mechanic of the outfit and made a big play for Marie. The men escorted them to the Commission of Arms in *Nacaome* where they were required to report, but all was routine. While relaxing over a beer, the decision was made to have a joint dinner. Smokey and Persh went to the base and got eggs, the girls pitched in to fix whatever was available, and a feast was enjoyed by lantern light. The soldiers brought two quarts of Canadian Club which quickly disappeared. An invitation to park at the camp overnight was readily accepted. Smokey showed them all the equipment they used for road-building, then took Marie for a ride in his jeep. They drove to *San Lorenzo* and had a beer. On the way back he stopped to show her the river they swam in. They returned to the camp at midnight. Everyone there was already in bed and they all enjoyed a marvelous night's sleep.

At 6:00 a.m. the sounds of trucks rumbling by and soldiers on morning drill served as a wake-up call. Soon Ed appeared with a big tray of scrambled eggs and tomatoes and a huge pot of coffee. Smokey and Ben adjusted the valves and tappets on the car, then Smokey conducted a tour of the town in

his Jeep and picked up two bottles of liquor. From that point on, time dissolved in a boozy haze. Marie described the day as a lost Friday. They ate and drank, went to the river and swam, then headed for *San Lorenzo*. Eileen passed out, ended up in the car with Pic and Jan and awoke at dusk at an Esso Station in *San Lorenzo* thinking it was the next morning. Persh was in even worse shape, and everyone was dragging. The Army men were passing out aspirin right and left. Pic and Jan were disgusted and took off in the truck. They all now headed to *Choluteca;* Persh, Babe, and Eileen rode with Ben in the Jeep, Smokey was with Marie in the car. Ben took a shortcut, rough and bumpy, skidding and sliding, over a lot of bridges and through several streams. Then a huge black cloud opened up and poured torrents on them. The streets in *Choluteca* were like a river, and the starter on the Jeep went out. Ben got a room at a pension, but the other five tried to sleep jammed into the car as they waited by the bridge on the highway for Pic and Jan to show up in the truck.

In the morning, they ate breakfast at the pension where Ben had stayed, then began a search for the two girls. Men who were working on the bridge had to lay down special boards for the car to cross, but the truck with Pic and Jan was parked by the roadside a short distance on the other side. Once the group was united, goodbyes were said to Ben and Smokey who had to return to base, and the journey south continued. A wide gravel road started its climb up to 4,500 ft., but sixteen miles from the border it petered out into a very narrow gravel road with occasional muddy places on steep hills. Honduras had an exceptionally impressive new customs house at the border and the agents were very accommodating---one of them spoke some English. Ted had been there and left a note saying he probably wouldn't see them again. A short way ahead, at the bottom of a hill, they were stopped to show their passports at a gateway entrance to Nicaragua.

Chapter 12: Welcome to Nicaragua

<u>Saturday, May 22.</u> A short distance after passing through the gate, they saw Ted trudging along the road so they picked him up and proceeded to the customs house in the town of *Somoto.* There their suitcases were unloaded and they received the unwelcome news that, because it was Saturday, the work crew had to be paid US$3 for overtime. After repacking the bags, they were sent to the General, waited for him to sign their passports and were charged another $3 for overtime. They had no Nicaraguan money and no U.S. dollar bills, but someone came up with the money and they were off to find a camping spot as they were advised not to try the mountains after dark. Ted left them after he found a truck that would give him a ride to *Managua.* A splendid camping place was found beside a creek, under large trees, and they were able to do some laundry before having an early dinner. Two guests visited during dinner asking for cigarettes and money. It was a lovely moonlit evening, but they were pestered with mosquitos and chiggers all night long.

<u>Sunday, May 23.</u> Next morning, the sheets were bloody from mosquito bites. The creek came alive with stunning butterflies, pale green, yellow, orange, white, black-and-white striped; also pretty birds resembling the blue jays and red-headed woodpeckers back home and one with a strange song like a faraway frog. Three uninvited locals showed up for breakfast but since provisions were in short supply they were not invited to share, and a small crowd, including a burro, gathered to watch the campers pack and leave. The road ahead up the mountains was narrow with a few muddy spots but not too challenging. For a short while they were accompanied by a group of six macaws flying noisily overhead. When they arrived at *Estelí,* they searched for *Señor Montinegra,* said to be the owner of a theater there who was to change some money for them. They ran into a local man who owned a big ranch, had gone to school at Cornell and knew the man they were looking for. He took them to the theater-man's

home where the sister and mother entertained them by playing the piano while waiting for *Señor Montinegra* to show up. He was leaving for California the next morning but, once he arrived, he changed some money (six *cordobas* per dollar) and invited them to attend his theater that evening. They declined the invitation as they wanted to get on a paved highway because it was beginning to rain heavily. Gas was expensive in *Estelí* so, down the road, during a pause in the downpour, they put five gallons of their own gas in the cars, the first time they had used any of it. The countryside was now very flat and getting greener. Lake *Managua* lay a few miles to the west on their right but remained out of sight. Then, without even realizing it, they were surprised to find themselves in the city of *Managua,* situated right at the south end of the lake. On this Sunday afternoon the town seemed very quiet except for the countless horse-and-carriage taxis. They shopped for a place to stay and settled on the Gran Hotel, room and meals for C$5. The hotel had a nice lobby, dining room, and pool. The rooms were large but not very clean and poorly furnished. The beds were terrible. Still it was the first time they had enjoyed a hotel stay since Guatemala City. Everybody checked in, went for a swim, then went down to dinner at 8:30 and learned that the dining room closed at 8:30, but they were served anyway and the food was good. Afterwards they had *refrescos* at a nearby delicatessen and ran into Ted who was all dressed up and had been to their hotel looking for them. They all went to a movie, then retired to their rooms. Marie was up half the night doing laundry, ironing, and *"getting myself resurrected"*.

Monday, May 24. The necessary rounds were made, first to the National Palace to report, then to customs house to check the cars in. They looked up the address that Mr. Griffin had given them in El Salvador to learn about sending the cars by boat and found Mr. Phillips. He was very helpful, showed them a relief map of the area ahead. He told them they would not be able to drive to San Jose, Costa Rica, because a stretch of about 15 miles of road was barely passable in the dry season, and now that the rainy season had been underway for a month, it would at best be passable only by being pulled through with oxen. He gave several suggestions. The best option, they decided, was to talk to Mr. Guzman, a cattleman with experience in shipping boatloads of cattle from *San Juan del Sur* and who was staying at their hotel. Coincidentally, when they returned to the hotel Mr. Guzman walked in just as they were getting the keys to their rooms. He did not speak English well so he called in a co-owner of the boat, an American girl named Ann Madden. They held an impromptu conference right there in the lobby. He quoted a price of US$100 for each car and $25 per person unless the group wanted to camp out on deck which was okay with them. Twenty cattle would have to be taken off the boat to make room. But after lunch the price changed to a total of $280 which was negotiated down to $260. The boat was scheduled to depart for Panama from *San Juan del Sur* on Wednesday so everybody scurried to pack and check out. Ted arranged a trip to Panama by plane and said he would meet them Saturday morning at the dock there. Accompanied by Mr. Guzman and Ann, the troop headed south. The trip to *Rivas* took longer than they expected even though the road was good most of the way. The first thing they did when they arrived in *Rivas* was to check the road to *San Juan del Sur*. Everyone said it was impassable because of the heavy rains and a river

that had to be forded. When they accompanied Mr. Guzman and Ann to the Gran Central Hotel, they learned that something had broken on the boat that morning and repairs would take at least four days. Mr. Guzman bought dinner for everyone at the hotel and, after an evening of cordial conversation, the group camped near the hotel and fell asleep while being serenaded by a man with a mandolin and a very pleasant voice.

Tuesday, May 25. Pic, Jan, and Ann took the 7:00 a.m. train to *San Juan del Sur*. Marie, Babe, and Eileen had breakfast at the hotel. As they were leaving, Babe spied a middle-aged professional-looking man in the lobby. On a hunch, she approached him. "Pardon me, sir," she said, "but do you speak English"?

Chapter 13: The Rivas Family

Rivas is an important name in Nicaragua. A state (*departamento*), the city, and at least one president have been named Rivas. It was logical to assume that the city was named after an early ancestor of Dr. Rivas. That was true, but the relationship was actually quite distant since the lineage spanned 228 years[1], more than ten generations.

Marie described their experiences with the Rivas family in the following entry in her journal:

"The second day we were here in Rivas, we met a family whose name is Rivas. We were told that the city was named after their great grandfather who was the first President of Nicaragua. Dr. Rivas (the man Babe met in the hotel lobby) is a dentist, studied in the U. S. and speaks English quite well. He and his wife have seven children. The oldest boy, Johnny, is 22 and has been going to college in Managua and plans to leave in August for Boulder, Colorado, to study medicine there. He has a tremendous crush on me which has been a very interesting experience. He speaks some English and has been learning it fast since we arrived. They are a very nice family and have been so wonderful and helpful to us. Johnny has been with us almost every minute and is like one of the family. He is about as nice as they come and we all like him very much. If the people down here like you, they will do almost anything under the sun for you. We didn't have a place to stay. There are several hotels in town but we couldn't afford to stay in one and none of them is very appealing anyway. But the Rivas family has a ranch located a couple of miles out of town so they took us there to stay with them. Because of the muddy road, we had to leave the cars about a mile from the house and trudge through the mud several times a day because we usually sleep in the cars. Otherwise the place is great. It's located right on Lake Nicaragua. They have a canoe that we take out for fishing, horses to ride (we often ride them back and forth to the cars),

servants to do all the work, a woman who is half Indian-half Negro to do the cooking. The main dishes here are black beans, boiled rice (sometimes fried), and fried bananas which are on the table almost every meal including breakfast. Persh and I caught some fish and gave them to the cook to fry, but when she brought them to the table they smelled bad and we saw that she had just scraped off some of the scales and put the fish in the skillet---head, insides, and all. We have set up our little stove and cooked some American food occasionally. The ranch also has a woods full of monkeys. There are two different kinds---the big, black, chubby Congo type that just sits, grunts, and looks at you, and the tall slim yellowish ones with a black face. They are pretty and graceful, much more active and interesting to watch as they jump and swing around in the trees by their tails".

Chapter 14: Stranded in Rivas

Wednesday, May 26. A man was supposed to wake Persh and take him to meet Mr. Guzman at the train at 8:00 a.m., but he never showed up. The rain started mid-morning and poured off and on all day. They made their way back to the Rivas ranch where they sat, drank coffee, talked, and slept. It was a surprisingly cold and generally nasty day. Johnny and Marie went horseback riding in between downpours. Later Persh and Johnny got out the canoe, put on their bathing suits, and went fishing in the lake (Lake Nicaragua[14]) but saw mainly sharks and turtles. After an early dinner, the travelers returned to the cars and had a very good night's sleep.

The sun was shining brightly when they awoke the next morning. The girls hung their laundry out to dry and it immediately started to rain. The day was spent at the ranch, Marie sleeping, Persh fishing. He caught enough for dinner which Pic and Jan prepared. After dinner, Dr. Rivas took a group crabbing down at William Walker's 100-year-old ship[14-A]. They caught seven crabs, saw five snakes and a skunk and got very muddy in the process. Everyone except Persh and Eileen stayed at the ranch overnight. Next morning, they all gathered for breakfast at the hotel, after which Dr. Rivas took them to see a man about a boat but nothing came of it. Then back to the ranch for a lazy afternoon resting, sleeping, and fishing. They slept in the cars that night and were awakened by a torrential deluge.

Back at the ranch next morning, Persh and Marie had some success at fishing while the others went to town. Everyone returned by 5:00 p.m., had venison for dinner, and then lazed around. Marie and Johnny cuddled in a hammock, Pic, Jan and Eileen wrote letters, Babe listened to the radio and watched for scorpions. At 8:00 p.m., Persh and Dr. Rivas decided to go deer hunting. It was too late to fetch the horses so they drove a ways, then walked into the jungle under a waning gibbous moon. They saw four deer, some within 40 feet of them, but all four ran away before the hunters could get off a shot, largely due to Dr. Rivas's excited jabbering and wanting to get closer before shooting. Two raccoons were playing in a puddle of water and didn't even look up as the animals had no fear of humans. Besides the deer and coons, they saw possums, skunks, whippoorwills, frogs, and toads.

Early the next morning, Persh and Eileen walked into the forest to look for monkeys. They hadn't gone far before they saw a big black monkey staring at them, letting out an occasional grunt. In a nearby tree were eight black monkeys, two with babies; they didn't move but began to chant at the intruders. Babe and Marie came to take in the sight. A little further on, a group of spider monkeys, yellow with a black face, put on a entertaining show, climbing onto bare limbs, jumping from limb to limb and tree to tree, hanging by their tails. The forest was getting hot so the visitors took an ox trail back to the house, passing native huts along the way. A swim in the lake cooled them down after which they enjoyed a late breakfast of pancakes at the house. Two local men, Carlos and Jorge, came to relay a message from Mr. Guzman that the boat wouldn't be ready for at least a week. Carlos was a rancher, and Jorge was studying to be a doctor and spoke English quite well. Their jeep got stuck in the driveway so everybody helped to push it out. After they left, Pic and Jan went fishing, Marie and Johnny rode horses into town. Persh climbed a coconut tree, picked six coconuts and skinned his legs up badly. Then he and Dr. Rivas went deer hunting and returned at 4:00 a.m. with no deer. They had joined a hunting group that rode into the jungle on horseback. Persh, who was unaccustomed to riding horseback, said that he "*damned near fell off the horse when he mounted it*", that the horseback ride was sheer torture on a trail that was wet and slippery. The horse would slip on rocks, stumble over logs, at times up to his belly in mud, with Persh hanging on for dear life. Thorns, sticks, and limbs scratched and tried to pull him out of the saddle. They forded rivers, climbed steep hills, went down steeper ones in a steady downpour, finally meeting up with another party that had killed three deer. A wealthy man in that party had a fifth of Scotch that he compassionately shared with Persh who vowed that henceforth he would only hunt alone, on foot, and with his pistol.

Persh's leg didn't get attended to until they returned to the cars the next morning. That day, Marie and Johnny drove to *Managua* to apply for a passport for Johnny. While in *Managua*, they stopped at the Gran Central Hotel for a snack and met an elderly couple from Marlin, Texas, who were excited to meet Marie. They said that all along their trip they had heard a lot about this group of "University girls" from the U.S. and the courageous journey they were making. Apparently the name came from the fact that Marie often wore a University of Wisconsin T-shirt. The Texans were Dr. and Mrs. Bolivar Lang Falconer. He was the first paying customer to fly around the world entirely by air and in 1937 wrote a book about it: "Flying Around the World". They gave Marie an El Salvadoran coin as a remembrance. She and Johnny returned to the ranch around noon. At 4:00 p.m., Persh and Johnny left in the car to get Dr. Rivas and got the car stuck in a swampy area. When they positioned the truck around to pull it out, the truck got stuck, too. Then it started to rain. Two hours later it was dark and, despite a concerted effort by all, both cars were still stuck in the mud. They hoofed it back to the ranch for dinner and stayed all night. During the night, a huge bat with a wing span of 30 inches got into the house and scared everybody. When it started flying around the ceiling, Johnny grabbed a broom, chased it from room to room and finally brought it to the floor with a good hit. It was a very ferocious, ugly-looking thing, identified as a vampire bat, very harmful to cattle as it sucks their blood---as the name suggests. Persh added its skull to his collection.

Tuesday, June 1. The whole group, working in the rain with pulleys until 2:30 p.m., got the car out but not the truck even when they used the car for pulling. Working in a steady cold rain, they all got soaked to the skin, eventually gave up. They put on warm dry clothes and went to town in search of a gravel truck, ending up at the hotel for a big dinner. There they met Carlos and Jorge who introduced them to Eugene Maurice, a large rancher, who offered to bring oxen the next day. Carlos told them about a vacant house that might be available for them to stay in, a government-owned structure that had been built by the American government and occupied by engineers who constructed the local section of the Pan American Highway. It was a perfect set-up, right on Lake Nicaragua with a gravel road right up to the door and electricity in the evenings. It was well built, like an army barracks with one large room in front and three more rooms in back. Approval was needed from Mr. Maurice who had local control of the house because it was on his property. He readily agreed and formally extended the offer which was immediately accepted. They decided to use only the large room in front to set up their

beds and kitchen. Mr. Maurice gave them canvas cots to use and they brought their mattresses in from   the truck and were very comfortable. It gave them a sense of freedom in that they weren't imposing on anyone. Dr. Rivas didn't want them to move from his ranch. Eileen thought it was *through pure jealousy* but it was more likely that he was just being protective of his flock. He told them that Maurice ran with a bad gang that had wild parties at that place and they'd be bothered with people and couples with ill-intent coming at all hours. Apparently the vacant house had a reputation for being used for late night rendezvous.

The next morning, Carlos showed up after breakfast with a gang and four oxen to pull the truck out but couldn't budge it. Johnny rounded up two more oxen from somewhere and, with all six pulling and using a block and tackle, they finally succeeded, pulling a tree over in the process. The truck left a huge hole in the ground after setting for two days with almost constant rain. Numerous sessions of wheel-spinning had sunk it in so deep it was setting on the spare-tire rack on its rear end. In a spirit of relief, everybody adjourned to the new house, unpacked the truck, washed it and dusted out the inside so it looked respectable again. Carlos and Jorge came by and joined them for their first dinner in their new home. That night they discovered that the house was also home to some rats and scorpions.

A scorpion was found in one of Babe's shoes on the truck, a fact that was concealed from Babe for fear she would never get in the truck again. These scorpions were alleged to be not very poisonous but their bite could make people sick with 'trembles" and swollen tongues. Johnny let one sting him to show that it didn't hurt that much. To protect against the scorpions in the night, Persh put up hammocks completely enclosed with mosquito netting for Babe and Marie to sleep in. The first night Marie had just got all comfortably settled in her hammock when she suddenly found herself on the floor---the nails had come out of the wall, leaving her with a sore tail-bone for a few days.

A mandatory trip to *Managua* was on the docket next day. Dr. Rivas and Johnny joined them, and they all piled into the truck and drove through pouring rain to reach the National Palace. There they met the foreign minister who extended their stay to thirty days. At lunch at the hotel they met Mr. Guzman and Ann and learned there would be no boat for at least thirty days. Dr. Rivas insisted on taking them to visit a cousin, a former mayor of *Managua*. Supposedly one of the wealthiest families in *Managua*, their home was quite simply but typically furnished: a table in the center of a room with a circle of wicker or straight, uncomfortable chairs around it. The family, however, was very warm and welcoming. The doctor took them to see a monument to his cousin placed in a park along the waterfront. Dr. Rivas said the cousin built and paid for the monument himself. From there they hastened through dinner in order to catch a movie, 'Sea of Grass' with Katherine Hepburn and Spencer Tracy which they expected to be in English but wasn't. After the show Dr. Rivas wanted to eat at the *Bonbonniers* where he and a waitress had a noisy misunderstanding about the cook. It was 2:30 a.m. when they finally returned to Rivas.

Friday, June 4. At this point, the girls now found themselves with time on their hands and not much to do as they had to wait until suitable boat passage could be scheduled. Their time was spent washing their clothes, washing their hair, bathing in the lake, fishing, shopping, writing letters, and sunning. Persh, on the other hand, was in his element: a Central

American jungle right outside his doorstep and night after night to hunt and explore. On this night's outing, he went into the jungle near the border with Costa Rica. It was dark and raining so he gave himself an hour to find something. He saw no deer but as he was coming back he saw eyes about 50 feet away, low to the ground. As they came closer, he could tell it was a large cat. A single pistol shot took the animal down. It was an ocelot, a female of about 50 pounds with a beautiful clean coat of fur.

The next day he skinned his "tiger" and stretched the fur, then went day-hunting with some other men and came back with two albatrosses. That night, the girls went to an open-air movie expecting to see Errol Flynn in "Stormy Weather" in English but instead were shown Wallace Beery in Spanish. Afterwards they visited the Rivas Club for an evening of dancing, billiards, and card playing. On Persh"s nightly hunt, a possum walked right up to him and followed him around for quite a while----but no deer.

Monday, June 7. Johnny took Persh to a tanning place that showed him how to tan his ocelot skin, a 30-day process that required unbleached muslin and chemicals that were available from the drugstore. Pic and Jan went fishing in the river, Marie and Johnny rode horseback into town to get medicine for a sick cow, Eileen did laundry in the lake, and Persh and the doctor went hunting in mid-afternoon. There had been no meat in the local market that morning, so Maurice brought over a dozen eggs and two chickens. They had just started to eat dinner when the lights went out. Then the lantern mantle blacked out, so they ate dinner in the dark and went to bed early. The hunters returned empty-handed once again.

While on the river (*Rio de Oro*) a day later, Persh shot three iguanas, one measuring 62 inches tail-to-toe. Then they observed something swimming across the river----binoculars showed it to be a 12-foot long alligator that swam parallel to their boat but not near enough to shoot. After dark, Persh and Eileen walked to the river and used a big row boat belonging to Maurice to hunt for that big alligator. They saw eyes on shore and shot a strange animal----half-rabbit/half-pig with splendid soft brown fur with white stripes and spots. They later learned it was a *paca,* locally called tepezcuintle, said to be choice eating. They took it home and dressed it out to be eaten next day for dinner. At a shallow place in the river, the boat passed under trees where white heron were roosting, making a sound like pigs  grunting and splattering the water with their excrement. Eileen surmised that the birds had eaten too much Ex-Lax; thankfully the boat was not doused. Coming back upstream Persh got a 4-foot-long alligator. They returned home exhausted at 3:30 a.m. without sighting the big alligator.

Marie and Jan went to the market early the next morning and came back with some beef. It was tough but beef was hard to find in Rivas. Vegetables were also hard to come by except for cabbage. Carrots were 30¢ each. Some natives gave Babe an adorable parrot, green and blue with red wingtips; it was a lora parrot so she named it Lorito,  It had been a pet and was accustomed to being tied by a string to her perch but *"no habla"*. The house had also become home to two stray dogs, Ranger and Valentino, who chased the hogs and vultures away. Eileen made friends with Taversé, a little woman who lived nearby; she said she would iron their clothes for a small fee. Eileen gave her six pieces to try and they came back beautifully done. Taversé was amazed at all the traveler's possessions, the camp stove, the lantern, the hammocks, everything. She wanted Persh to take her picture but had a hard time conveying to him what she wanted. She became fixated on Marie and her possessions: wanted her shoes and the little sewing machine and ironing board that Marie had brought along. She wanted Marie to fix her skirt and make her a dress like a yellow one that Marie wore. But when Marie fixed her skirt, she complained about the result. Taversé had a big oven so she roasted the "pig" that Persh and Eileen had shot the night before. Mr.

Maurice came for dinner, then he and Persh went hunting at 10:00 p.m. Persh shot two rabbits and a fox and came home with a live alligator about 2-feet long but it lived for only a day or two.

Thursday, June 10. The girls went into Rivas to get permits to enter Costa Rica. Then they all went to the border about 30 miles south which was marked by an old stone monument showing the flags of Nicaragua and Costa Rica side-by-side and bearing an inscription that was too eroded to read. Marie approached the monument and, as if translating, read loudly *"This monument marks the spot where the Pan American Highway to South America died."* Her words rang true as there was nothing but a winding path ahead, muddy as a pig pen. A short way down the path was a mad, raging river, quite deep in spots as they could tell by watching men ride across on horseback. They were told the "road" was this bad or worse for 40 kilometers ahead and in this stretch there were 30 rivers to cross, some deeper than this one, with no bridges and more rain to be expected as the road rose into the mountains. A local fellow quipped that it was impossible for even a bird. They noticed that the landscape there was much greener with more wild growth than in the Rivas area. They returned back to the house and had rabbits for dinner. Johnny slept in a hammock on the front porch and, despite Flit and flypaper, they all battled bugs all night long.

The next day there was a close encounter with Big Al, the big alligator. Pic and Persh left the house at 11:00 p.m. to go alligator hunting. They went way down the river in the boat, then walked down a ways further. They shot another *paca* and found a small pond with a dozen alligators in it but left to watch some black monkeys. On the way back they heard a terrific commotion right alongside the boat, next to the shore. It was Big Al. They quietly rowed the boat to the other side, sat and waited. Five minutes later, Big Al was seen coasting along the shore on the opposite side and stopped with his nose on the bank. Pic got out of the boat onto the bank, then Persh sneaked the boat across the river and got on shore on the other side. The gator wasn't where Persh expected him to be so he walked a ways up the bank while looking down at the river. When he came around a bend, there was Big Al smack dab in the middle of the river. Persh crouched down behind a clump of grass too small to conceal him and the gator headed right for him. Persh waited until Big Al was almost on him, then took a perfect bead on his eye. The gator made a terrific splash under the water which boiled for a few minutes, then all was quiet. That was the last seen of Big Al. Persh said the head was 14-inches across.

Succeeding days were spent in a fairly routine fashion. A couple of the girls would get up early in the morning to go to the local market and shop for food. Afternoons were generally quiet and hot, good for light chores and napping. They had met practically all the cream of Rivas society and had received numerous invitations to different ranches and affairs, but mostly they entertained themselves. Activity picked up after dark with late dinners, visitors stopping by, and nighttime hunting trips. Mr. Maurice came by every day, sometimes with food, sometimes bringing visitors, frequently to go hunting with Persh. Dr. Rivas was also a nearly-constant presence, resenting Maurice and belittling his efforts to entertain the visitors and make them feel comfortable. Eileen thought *"the doctor was so jealous it was pathetic"*. Johnny resonated back and forth between the house and the ranch, but for all practical purposes he lived at the house. He had developed a big crush on Marie and considered her "his girl". Persh went hunting every night with mostly poor luck except for rabbits, but they were always welcome.

Mr. Maurice

Dr. Rivas

Mr. Guzman

Carlos

Lake Nicaragua in the background

One night Maurice invited them to his ranch for soup, but when they arrived they were told it was all gone except for a couple of tiny cupsful that sat on the table, and the fellows passed it from one to the other. Finally Persh tasted it but Maurice told him not to eat it because it wasn't clean. It turned out that the soup was made from freshly killed housecat. Two days later Dr. Rivas told them he heard that they had eaten cat soup at Maurice's ranch and everyone in town knew about it and was laughing at them. He was furious that Maurice had pulled such a trick on them, but they laughed and said they had always wanted to taste cat soup which infuriated the doctor.

Wednesday, June 16. In talking amongst themselves, the girls concluded that Persh was in no hurry to leave this area. They decided that they needed to take the initiative in finding transportation out of Nicaragua. At 6:00 a.m., they drove with Johnny to *Managua* to seek information about catching a boat. While they were gone, Persh and Eileen took a long walk along the river to commemorate their fifth wedding anniversary. They found a peaceful spot, sat for a long time enjoying the beauty of their surroundings, watching the parrots, fish, ducks, cranes, turtles and all manner of riparian wildlife. Coming back, they came across the carcass of a cow that had become stuck in the mud; crows had eaten her eyes out and the cow died. Now the vultures had picked the carcass clean to the bone. A fifth anniversary dinner consisted of corned beef, potatoes, and beans. When the girls returned at 2:30 a.m., Persh got up and went hunting. The next night Eileen accompanied him, heading toward the border at 11:00 p.m. They saw two deer. Persh shot at one but missed. Skunks and rabbits were abundant. A pair of eyes in the dark turned out to be a little fox that they observed for ten minutes, then approached within two feet of him before he ran a few feet, stopped, sat, and looked back at them. The next night, the hunters returned to the same area and saw ten deer and an ocelot. Persh got off a few shots, hitting one deer but the gun jammed and, before he could deliver the coup de grace, the bleeding animal ran off into the jungle. He followed the bloody trail but the jungle growth was too thick to navigate so he gave up. Driving back home, Persh came to a sudden stop saying he saw eyes in a tree, very bright and high up. He crawled out to investigate and they both burst into laughter when they realized it was lights from a house in the distance.

In *Managua*, the girls were advised to go to *San Juan del Sur* and contact a man named Fisher who operated a launch to Costa Rica; also a man named Kelly who might be able to help in making arrangements for shipping the cars to Panama. In a letter home, Marie explained their long stay in Rivas: *"We were lined up to sail on a little cattle boat going directly from San Juan del Sur to Panama City, but the boat had to be dry docked for repairs. San Juan del Sur is only about 15 miles from here but the road is so bad that the only way we can get there is by shipping the cars by rail. None of the ships coming in there have a definite schedule so it is difficult to book passage or even know when the boats are going to arrive. There are two men at the port who are supposed to know such things so we check regularly with them. So far several boats have been in, but we couldn't get on any of them. There is another port, Puerto Corinto, 80 miles north of Managua which is said to be a larger port with more ships coming in, but to get there we need to ship the cars from Managua. Grace Lines and United Fruit dock there but they can't take passengers, so we would have to fly from there. We're also contemplating taking a ship directly to Peru, skipping Panama and Colombia, as they tell us that ships are not allowed to dock in Colombia at this time. But getting down to brass tacks, if we take a ship to Peru we would arrive in Lima with very little money, if any, and we would be up against it if we couldn't get jobs there. So we feel that the smartest thing to do is get jobs in Panama because we're pretty certain of getting employment there. But the political situation there is explosive and the cost of living will be high. It may be the end of our trip. We could possibly work in Managua but nobody is keen on it as they consider Managua to be a dull city".*

<u>Saturday, June 19.</u> The 7:30 a.m. train to *San Juan del Sur* was tiny but clean. Travel time was a little more than an hour for a trip of 21 kilometers (13 miles) through interesting countryside with thick growth in places.

They found *San Juan* to be a beautiful little port set back in a bay with high cliffs all around. The beach was very clean and calm and the water was very clear and blue. Upon arrival, they went to the hotel and met with Mr. Fisher, the man with the launch. He wanted C$400 to take them to *Puerto Jiménez* near the Panama border in Costa Rica, but his launch seemed too light a boat to carry two heavy cars. Mr. Kelly was a jolly fat man with a large family who happened to be a Panamanian consul. He told them that he was the wrong person to help them. The man they needed to see was Mr. Holmann who turned out to be a youngish man, small in stature. His

family was reputed to be the second wealthiest in Nicaragua, but he had a common air about him with twinkling eyes and a warm personality. He said that if Guzman ordered him to take twenty cows off, they could leave for Panama on Tuesday. But, aside from the possibility of earning some money there, Panama was not the ideal destination because the Pan America Highway did not continue through Panama to Colombia, so they would have to ship the cars again by boat to Ecuador or Peru. Mr. Holmann mentioned that there were two or three other boats coming in soon, one going to Peru. He sent a cable asking the price for passage as a special favor for him. The group returned to the hotel, then went for a swim in the delightful blue Pacific Ocean. It was wonderfully refreshing with perfect waves and, though the water was cold, the sun was hot. Jan and Johnny sought out Mr. Johnson, the Peruvian consul, to get a price for entering the cars in Peru. They all had lunch at the hotel, then caught the 2:00 p.m. train back to Rivas.

On the return trip, the train was full with natives and their kids, loading their wares in baskets, bundles, and boxes. There were a dozen horse-and-buggy taxis to meet the train when it arrived in Rivas. The truck had been left at the station so they made a quick trip to the hotel to quench their thirst with a Coke, drove to the Rivas ranch to pick grapefruit and limes, returned to town for a Saturday night luncheon of cheese, pork tamales, and fresh-baked bread, and declined an invitation to a dance in someone's home. Despite the fact that sleep-deprivation had caught up with them, all but Marie and Babe decided to go hunting. Pic drove the truck, Eileen sat in the back and snored so loud they accused her of scaring off the game. At midnight they parked in the jungle and everybody napped for a couple of hours, after which the hunt resumed, resulting in the shooting of three rabbits.

Marie and Babe were up early the next morning to wash dishes and clean house. Marie had bought some fish and potatoes from Taversé to serve for brunch when the others finally got up. She was not interested in their hunting trips; in fact she did not approve of killing innocent wild animals although she did acknowledge that the game had provided them with some good meals. After brunch, they all adjourned to the Rivas ranch. Mr. Holmann reported that he had not yet heard back from Peru. Several attempts to contact Mr. Guzman were unsuccessful. The afternoon was spent in food, drink, and hijinks. A local lady sang *"Managua, Nicaragua"* which was very popular at that time. Dr. Rivas was taught some toasts in English; the one he liked best was improvised on the spot: "Here's to Eat". The doctor had some mamons (Spanish limes), an odd fruit that grows in clumps and whose flesh clings to a large seed. To eat them, one bit the skin open, then sucked out the whole insides. It felt like an eyeball but tasted sweet, tart and juicy! Persh and Eileen went hunting. Eileen drove the truck and Persh would get out in certain spots to look for deer. At one stop, she heard Persh shoot repeatedly. He had shot at a female deer, missed her but shot her fawn by mistake. The doe returned to look for her baby but the pistol jammed on his best shot at her. They felt bad about killing the fawn: *"he was so cute with a fat little tummy"*. Nevertheless, they dressed him out and Taversé cooked him in her oven with a sauce.

Pic and Jan returned to *San Juan* the next morning to find that Mr. Guzman had gone to Panama and Mr. Holmann still had no response from Peru so all was on hold for the present. That evening everybody but Persh and Eileen went to town and had drinks and dinner at a new place opened by Tobe, "*a Negro from San Juan. Tobe was very pleasant and interesting; he spoke perfect English and was clever at food*". Some local men walked by and saw them there, then went to the Rivas Club and told Dr. Rivas who rushed over and told them they should leave at once as they were with a rough crowd. Johnny's temper sometimes got aroused by drink. Jan was driving back to the house with him in a jeep and, when they were stopped by an army guard on the highway, Johnny urged her to drive on through despite the fact that the guard had his gun aimed at them. Jan went back to headquarters and got a pass. This was not the only encounter that Johnny had with army guards who were patrolling the highways. Political discontent was in the air in Nicaragua, and it was rumored that revolution would break out at any time but nobody knew when or where.

Wednesday, June 23. Señor Maurice came to invite them to listen to the Louis-Walcott fight that was being broadcast at 8:00 p.m., but when they got there they heard that the fight had been postponed due to rain in New York. They ended up at Tobe's new place where they danced to a four-piece orchestra that played their requests for favorite songs. The lights went out at 11:00 so they continued by candlelight. Maurice insisted on paying the bill for everyone and everything including cigarettes. Babe, Persh, and Eileen went hunting after they returned to the house. It was 3:00 a.m. when they returned with no deer, but Persh had shot two rabbits.

The next day Carlos and some friends came with a bottle of Scotch just as Babe and Eileen were leaving to take Persh hunting. They dropped him off and when they returned, about an hour later, the Scotch was nearly gone. Alfredo, one of the fellows, promised Babe a monkey. Maurice came by with a chicken, some cheese, and an invitation to a dance in town. After a dinner of chicken and yucca, they picked up Persh who had shot two deer!

Persh spent the next day cutting up deer meat and gave most of it away to Taversé, Mr. Maurice, and the doctor. Alfredo Urcayo, the fellow who promised Babe a monkey, invited everyone to a party at his ranch, *Napalapa* at *San Jorge*, a nearby town. He was sporting a new amphibious jeep; some of them rode in it and the rest went in the car, bouncing over a bumpy road to get there. When they arrived, men were opening a huge bunch of coconuts on the front steps. The house was lovely, very large with a big porch overlooking Lake Nicaragua and a good beach area with clean sand. They were served shrimp and drinks with coconut juice. Jose, a friend of Alfredo's, serenaded them with guitar music. Alfredo picked red and white roses for the ladies to wear to the dance that evening and later presented Babe with a capuchin monkey named Alfredo Pechardo Urcayo. When they got back to the house, Persh conked out from too little sleep and too much to drink so they went to the dance without him. The hostess had provided a bountiful buffet and wonderful drinks. The orchestra started to play and the girls danced, mostly with Dr. Rivas, Johnny, Jorge, Maurice, and Alfredo. The lights  went out so they danced by the light of a kerosene lamp. After nearly everyone else left, the orchestra went wild playing every kind of dance music: square dance, marches, tangos, waltzes, congas, rhumbas, while the dancers used their imaginations to improvise steps that no one could ever have recognized. Dr. Rivas was furious when he heard that Persh got drunk at the ranch and that Jose had kissed all the girls. He nearly got into a fight with Jose over it but declared that they would fight a duel instead.

The next several days were spent in limbo. The girls washed and simonized the cars which took more physical effort than they had had for weeks. They kidded Babe about adding two new members to the Pickens family: Lorito, the parrot, and Alfredo, the monkey. Babe was spending most of her time waiting on them and playing with them. The parrot tended to have an unpleasant disposition, but the monkey was everybody's favorite. The others were amused at how Babe had gotten so attached to her pets, but no one thought she would even consider taking them along to Chile. But she had a cage built for the parrot and a crate for the monkey and had every intention of taking them along. The rest of the group eventually agreed to it because she enjoyed them so much and it kept her mind occupied so she didn't get so concerned when things turned sour. So they spent their time playing with the monkey, eating, drinking, and writing letters. Mail from

home took a week to arrive. On successive days, Johnny brought a bottle of rum; Jorge, Carlos, and Alfredo brought a bottle of Scotch which they drank while discussing the tense situation between Dr. Rivas and Jose. Maurice brought a bottle of rum and proposed to Pic who was somewhat taken aback but composed herself and politely declined; he then drank what was left of the rum and left. Marie and Johnny came back from grocery shopping with a bottle of *Bate* to celebrate the news that

Marie's father had re-married on June 13th in Wisconsin (Marie's mother had died in 1946). *Bate* is a sugar cane rum, a traditional regional brew made with toasted chan (*hyptes suaveolens*) seeds. Marie described it as fire water that tasted a lot like tequila. Persh went hunting every night but one, saw plenty of deer but had to settle for rabbits.

Marie commented about the wildlife: *"This is a paradise for anybody who fully appreciates hunting and fishing. Persh is having the time of his life. He hunts so much that he can hardly find time to sleep—goes out practically every night and gets all sorts of things. He has gotten three deer so we're getting tired of venison. He has brought home several pacas that are considered a great delicacy down here but are not found in the States. It's small and fat with short legs, soft brown fur with white marks and no tail. They are good eating---taste like a delicate piece of pork. I am dying for green leafy vegetables. The rivers are full of alligators, fish, and giant lizards called eguanas---terrible looking things about 6 ft. long. On the lake there are all sorts of ducks, sea turkeys, herons, pink spoon-billed flamingoes, albatross, and vultures. Persh loves it so much he would like to come back here and live someday. Our view is enhanced by two volcanoes towering over the lake. They are islands in the lake and look near but are 9-10 miles away. Our present set-up is like being in a cottage on a lake in the Midwest, but we're afraid to swim in the lake because of the sharks and alligators".*

Thursday, July 1. Arrangements were being made to ship the cars to Peru on either the *Tarcoles* or the *Montoro,* but the sailing dates were uncertain. In any case, they had to get the cars down to *San Juan del Sur.* A test run was made of the road. It was passable for about a mile and could be walked on foot for about another mile, but beyond that the mud holes were gigantic, deep enough to bury a person. The road seemed angry, threatening to swallow them if they dared to venture onto it. So it became obvious that the cars would have to be shipped by rail to *San Juan.* On the way back they met a tremendous herd of cattle going to be loaded on the *Montoro.* Back at the house, Johnny brought a redheaded duck to be fixed for dinner and Taversé baked a cake which they topped off with a visit to Tobe's for ice cream.

Next morning they went in to Rivas to learn the reply to their cable requesting passage to Peru on the *Montoro.* The price quoted was $90 for 3rd class passage for each person plus $200 for each car. They decided that was too much so they would take the *Tarcoles* unless Mr. Guzman came up with something more affordable to Panama. Later in the afternoon they attended a 14th birthday party for Noah, Dr. Rivas's daughter. The crowd was mostly adults who were offered a splendid buffet with *Flor de Cana* rum. They were introduced to a game new to them where a jug covered with crepe paper was suspended from the ceiling with a string (piñata). Johnny pulled the string to move the jug up and down while a blindfolded person tried to hit it with a stick and break it. Everybody took their turn with the kids going first. Marie broke the stick in two but Babe broke the jug which, they discovered, meant the party was over. Everyone else left, but they were invited to stay for a delicious dinner and everybody ate heartily. It was a farewell dinner for the travelers since they would leave tomorrow for *San Juan*. Johnny accompanied them back to the house which they had named *Las Pachotes*. Everyone was busy packing for the trip next day, but Johnny sat on the porch with Marie until late hours discussing their relationship. With departure of the travelers for Peru looming, Johnny had been pressing for marriage and intimacy. Marie's musings on the tête-a-tête: *"Had a hard time fending him off but he was good, as usual. Johnny is really wonderful, as nice a fellow as you could possibly find. He seems to be very much in love with me----I think he would do anything for me. When he's a little older and has been in the States for a while, I'm going to be anxious to see him again. For some reason I can't think too much about marrying him although I do think it would be wonderful. We get along amazingly well together, everybody is crazy about him, and I do love him very much. I just wonder about the kind of lifestyle we might have"*

Saturday, July 3. Moving day! They packed the cars and were off. Lorito, the parrot, was put in her cage and anchored on the rear of the car. They bought a barrel suitable for the monkey. The girls stopped at a store to buy nails and ropes, then went to the railroad station. The vehicles were loaded on two flatcars using two planks on each. Spectators were amused at the girls wielding the heavy planks. Everything went smoothly. Then the girls went to the vet to get a certificate for Alfredo after which everybody went to eat at Dr. Rivas's. After dinner, Maurice took them back to the hotel where there was a big dance; he went into the kitchen and ordered special food for them. They had promised Tobe they would stop for ice cream, so they did----and overindulged; Pic pigged out with four dishes. Tobe had an orchestra there and served pigs in a blanket. No one wanted to leave, but eventually they returned to the hotel for a couple of rounds of beer back at the hotel, then returned to the station to sleep on the flatcars except for Marie who was with Johnny and wanted to stay at the hotel. It took a while to figure out what was going on at the station. There were hundreds of people milling around and, after more arrived, they went as one huge mass uptown to catch buses for *Managua*. The explanation was that under Somoza's rule, the government would pay the fare to *Managua* plus C$5.00 for each person to celebrate the Fourth of July as a way of keeping good relations with the United States. Somoza was not in office in 1948, but the practice continued. Fireworks went off all night at the Army Headquarters.

<u>Sunday, July 4</u>. They arose early and went to the Rivas's ranch to have coffee and say goodbye. Word reached them that the train was being held for them at the station, so a mad dash ensued. They could barely cough up enough money to pay for the cars and buy their tickets. Dr. Rivas finagled for them to ride free on the flatcars, so everybody hopped on, including Johnny, and the soot began to fly all over them as the train left the station. The man who told Dr. Rivas they could ride free came to collect their tickets and, despite Johnny's arguments, they had to fork over C$1.00 each.

Chapter 15: San Juan del Sur

<u>Independence Day</u>. They arrived in *San Juan* at 8:30 a.m. Persh backed the cars off the flatcars with the help of William, *"a very nice Negro who spoke English"*. Both cars came off safely and, before they were even unloaded and all the lumber returned, a party had started. Alfredo and his brother Ernest were at the hotel; they had just sent 900 cattle off to Peru on the *Montoro*. Also at the party were Mr. Johnson, the Peruvian consul; Tommy Thompson, Mr. Holmann's cousin; and Mr. Amoros, a Peruvian who was there to buy cattle to go on the *Montoro* which had just sailed. They had hors d'oeuvres and bottles of Scotch before a delightful dinner at the hotel. Alfredo paid all the bills which came to more than C$700. Mr. Holmann offered the travelers a house near his office. All the fellows from Rivas, including Johnny, returned home on the 4:00 p.m. train. Mr. Holmann showed them their new house which they settled into right away. It had been a very busy Fourth, but tiring, so they all went to bed early, wrapping themselves in sheets to protect against the mosquitos, listening to the noise of mangoes falling on the tin roof.

Meeting the 7:30 a.m. train from Rivas became the morning ritual, a last minute rush as they could hear the train blow its whistle coming around the bend. Everybody yelling: "Empty the basket," "Where's the money?," "Darn, there's no small change," "Get some onions," "Don't forget eggs," "Hurry up or there won't be anything left," "Where's the car keys?". There was always a mob of people there, either to buy food or to meet someone. The vendors on the train would unload baskets, bags, and bundles of fruits and vegetables through the windows, then set up shop alongside the train for people to buy them. Bananas were plentiful in Rivas but scarce in *San*

Juan. Onions and tomatoes were expensive, but citrus, squash, peppers, and other vegetables were cheap. The vendors never had change and, while waiting for it, the customers often lost the opportunity to buy something good at another stand.

The next few days were spent in killing time: writing letters, exploring the beach, fishing, hunting for shrimp and crabs with stops at the hotel for Pepsi and fruit drinks. Johnny rode his horse all the way over from Rivas. Roberto, a local boy, would bring his Spanish book and help them with their Spanish while he learned some English.

Thursday, July 8. Tommy Thompson came by to tell them that the Captain of the *Tarcoles* said their boat's crane couldn't handle the cars, and also the gate at customs in Panama was too narrow for the cars to drive through. A little later, Johnny reported that there had been a cable from Peru in answer to their inquiry of a few weeks earlier saying that the cars could be shipped on the *Rosarita* for $150 each along with two persons, but the other four would need to buy first class tickets. At the house, kids liked to come by to tease the monkey. Leon, a local fellow, helped Persh get checks cashed, then brought over a load of free groceries from his cousin's store. Later he chilled a bottle of wine that Alfredo from Rivas had given to the girls. The wine had come from Peru on the *Montoro*.

Next day, Marie, Persh, Johnny, and Babe went to the south rocks to spear lobsters but had no luck. They saw striking blue fish, a baby octopus, and many colorful shells. Roberto gave them several crabs that he had caught. Later Persh went diving for fish and came up with a fine lobster. Johnny left for home on his horse in a driving rain. Leon took everyone to the hotel for some beers and dinner. When they returned home, they were serenaded by a guitar and some pleasant voices.

Sunday, July 11. Leon came by early and said he was taking everybody fishing in a boat. They met Mr. Holmann, Mr. Guzman, and Alfredo at the hotel. There they piled into the car and into Mr. Holmann's jeep and headed for the dock. It was a hassle for the girls to get into the boat as it tipped and swayed so much. There was only enough fishing gear for five to fish at a time so some didn't get to fish at all. As they passed *El Faro*, the lighthouse on the coast, Alfredo caught a bonita, a type of tuna. The boat ventured south toward Costa Rica to *Punta Brasilito* and circled some big rocks. Marie was sure she saw monkeys on one of the rocks. Heading back, they sailed right through a large school of fish but none of them would bite. It started to rain and turned chilly so they returned to port with only moderate success in their fishing. Shortly after they got back to the house, Jan yelled out that people were shouting and running up the street, so they all rushed out to see what was going on. The story they heard was that one man had cut another man's wrist and the injured man had run to the Army headquarters, grabbed a rifle and shot the first man. Mr. Holmann came to the house in his jeep and asked if anyone wanted to see a man die. Babe and Marie volunteered but later regretted it. The man was shot through the neck and twice in the chest; he was still alive but very bloody. He died later. It was rumored that the Sergeant at Army headquarters took to the mountains because he felt it was his fault the man was killed. They fixed fish for dinner. Mr. Guzman, Alfredo, Leon, and Roberto came over after dinner and they studied Spanish all evening during which time Leon made a big play for Marie. The next day he was kidded by the others about being a bad boy. He said he would come back when Marie had finished the book she was reading.

On Tuesday, Alfredo took Persh fishing with three other men. They went north about a mile to the bay at *Playa Nacascolo*. The group caught a dozen albacore and five lobsters; Persh claimed two lobsters, an albacore, and a conch. He had a diving mask so he could see underwater. This was very popular with the boys----they all wanted to use it. When he returned home, Alfredo had a ball that belonged to the street kids. Persh took it away and the monkey became angry and bit him. Persh retaliated by spanking the little fellow. A bit later the monkey disappeared and they found him sitting in the middle of the street chattering and yelling at a circle of kids around him. Lobster was on the menu for dinner that night after which they studied Spanish with the usual crowd while Persh fixed his conch.

The next day was uneventful with fishing and sunning. Marie and Eileen shopped for groceries and found a nice-looking watermelon, but the potatoes were small and half rotten. Persh played checkers with Roberto and Alfredo who both cheated and got angry when they didn't win. Johnny arrived on his horse just as they finished dinner. Later he left to stable his horse at a nearby ranch and Marie drove over to bring him back to the house. Johnny reported that he was having trouble with his passport; Jessie James at the U.S. Consul told him that he would have to serve two years in the U. S. Army on an Immigrant Passport. Leon dropped in but left after seeing Johnny there. Lorito sat on the roof in the rain; when they got her down they thought she was bleeding from rat bites, but it turned out that getting her feathers wet had turned them dark.

Thursday, July 15. A group expedition was planned to go with William to *Nacascolo* to hunt for lobsters, but it was rained out. Persh and William went by themselves and returned with six, including two very large ones. William reported that the authorities had found the Army sergeant in the mountains. He had a machine gun and was with two other men; the one who had shot the man and the other who had fired two shots in the man's stomach as he lay dying. William said that they were now in jail in Rivas and one day they would be taken out of their cells for a walk and shot in the back. Despite the rain, Marie and Johnny went to the beach. Mr. Holmann came to tell them that the *Rosarita* would arrive soon as its crew was getting mail at *San Juan.* They ate the watermelon; it was delicious and the monkey enjoyed the seeds.

On his next visit to *Nacascolo,* Persh got another lobster, harpooned a handsome turtle, and caught a blowfish and a flathead: an odd-looking fish, flat with a weird head and big eyes. The blowfish was puffed up and spiny and used his tail as a rudder. Persh released him and swam along beside him just to watch his movements. The turtle had big scales on his shell, the kind that could be used for guitar picks.

There was a large Catholic parade on Saturday for Saint Carmen, saint of the seas. There were fireworks and band music with the crowd carrying a statue of a woman carrying a baby. Marie was nowhere to be found; Jan finally located her attending mass in the church. She was wearing slacks. That morning, Marie and Johnny had gone to see the aduana[22] about their passports as their 30-day extensions had expired. Pic, Jan, and Eileen went fishing and caught sand sharks.

Sunday, July 18. Marie, Johnny, Persh, and Eileen packed a basket and started out for *Toro* Bay, about a half-mile north of *Nacascolo*. From *Nacascolo* they took a wrong road, had to backtrack, then passed through a field of high grass which the hikers, clad in bathing suits and shorts, had a good deal of discomfort in traversing, but they eventually ended up at Toro Bay. The sand was littered with gorgeous shells. They saw many pretty fish, blue and white, black and yellow, blue and dark purple with blue heads. One area was a haven for sea urchins. There was a tall rock nearby that had the perfect face of an old lady with hair on top of her head. Johnny thought they could return by following the shoreline back to *Nacascolo*. First they tried a shortcut through the jungle where Eileen accidentally hit a wasp nest with her pole---she and Johnny were stung several times. The shortcut dead-ended so they had to go back to the shore. That route wasn't easy as they encountered a terrific steep rock at the promontory point with only tiny toe-holds, then across several gulleys pouring rushing water into the sea. Just when they thought they were home free, their path was obstructed by a huge rock with a steep vertical drop to the sea. There was a ledge that Persh and Johnny thought they could navigate, but the girls couldn't reach it. By now it was dark, but moonlit, and they had no choice but to retrace their footsteps and try a different approach. Marie and Eileen both fell on the slippery rocks and skinned their knees. Exhausted, they finally made it back to the beach at Toro Bay. They wanted to stay there all night, but Persh vetoed that idea saying that the others would worry about them and they would freeze wearing nothing but their wet bathing suits. They started out on foot and after a short distance came to a very steep dirt hill which Persh believed they needed to climb to reach the path they had taken on the way over. He climbed it and confirmed his belief, but the hill, being very nearly vertical, was a difficult climb for the others: they succeeded by crawling on their hands and knees and holding on to clumps of grass growing on the hillside for support. At the top was the field of grass they had struggled through on the way over. They then decided to head for the railroad tracks where they stopped to catch their breaths. Now on more familiar ground, they cut through Holmann's ranch, waded the *Rio Escondido* and were back at *San Juan*. Dinner never tasted so good after an exciting day when they wondered if they would ever see home again. They were thankful to have returned safely with only some wasp stings and a few skinned knees. Marie was especially lucky to have escaped being stung by the wasps as she was allergic to their venom. A sting could have put her in anaphylactic shock requiring immediate medical attention which, of course, was not available.

On Monday morning, Persh went fishing with Alfredo and came home with two big mackerel. At lunchtime Johnny walked in accompanied by a fellow with a scraggly beard and a very red nose, dressed in khaki, big straw hat, goggles, and high-top shoes. He said hello and announced that he was Nelson Taylor, taking a motorcycle trip to Panama during summer break from college at Seton Hall. He fit right in, was very friendly and very hungry. He had stayed in Rivas with the Holmann family the night before. Mr. Holmann told him that if he arrived in *San Juan* by 11:00 a.m., there were some beautiful American girls there with whom he could eat breakfast. He had ridden  his motorcycle down the railroad tracks and in so doing had broken his brake and footrest and had no lights. They talked him into staying all night, so they went to the beach where they were joined by Marie and Johnny who had been swimming in the river.

The next day all but Persh and Nelson took the train to Rivas to shop for groceries. They shopped at the market and at a couple of grocery stores in town. One gave them a big discount and another, Aritheo Cerda, asked what they wanted. Jan said they would like some fruit, and he said he would send a package to them in *San Juan del Sur* on the train with no charge. It arrived the next day. They stopped to see Dr. Rivas who was so happy to see them he left his anaesthetized patient sitting in the chair. He accompanied them back to the station with their groceries, paid for their hack, their fare, and the freight that the railroad charged them for taking a stalk of bananas. Persh met them at the *San Juan* station with the car.

They had no eggs for breakfast next morning so Nelson went out looking for some. After about an hour, he returned with two dozen. A boy came around selling turtle eggs so they bought some and fried one; it had very little white and the yolk tasted like meal. They all went to the beach and played football that ended in a tie when they were rained out. Eileen nagged Persh to get a haircut. The barber came to town three or four times a week with his little black bag, going from house to house. He was scheduled to be on Holmann's back porch that afternoon. Mr. Holmann told Persh where to go hunting on one of his ranches down toward Costa Rica, lent him his rifle and furnished a guide. Persh came home at 1:00 a.m. saying the moon was too bright for good hunting. They only saw skunks and some rat-like animal. After hunting, they had gone for a swim toget rid of chiggers and were awed by the beauty of the phosphorescence as they swam in the moonlit waters of the Pacific.

Pic woke Persh up early the next morning saying the monkey was loose and causing havoc in Holmann's store where he was eating candy and scaring people. Persh was able to restrain and chain the little guy. In the late afternoon, the boys went rabbit hunting with Mr. Holmann and Tommy. They returned with nine rabbits. Marie made potato soup and played cards with Nelson and Persh after dinner.

Friday, July 23. A small group took Nelson to *Nacascolo* to hunt for lobsters. They caught seven and were distracted by an octopus and some sea cucumbers, elongated and cylindrical creatures that appeared to consist of blue jelly. The incoming tide forced the group into the nearby woods where they looked for monkeys but saw instead a family of anteaters with long striking brown-and-black fur, long bushy tails, and distinctively long noses. The mother had eight young ones that approached within four feet of the spectators before scattering. Some of the young ones ran up a tree.

It rained really hard on Saturday, but a boat whistle was heard above the rain. It was the *Chilikee*. The boys went down and watched them load cattle onto the barge that took the cattle to the boat. Sunday arrivals on the morning train from Rivas included Johnny and Mr. Holmann's brother, Irazno. Marie was there to pick up Johnny. Irazno announced that he was taking everybody fishing on Mr. Holmann's boat. All but Marie and Johnny went on the fishing expedition which was quite successful. They caught 22 fish: mackerel, red snapper, rock fish, and something called gyral.

Monday, July 26. Nelson woke them up early to say goodbye. They had become quite attached to him and hated to see him go as he was always happy, singing, and busy, but they were never able to get him to shave his beard. A couple of days later he sent a note from Kelly's Ranch near the border with a cute poem that sounded as if he was ready to give up on completing his trip to Panama. Mr. Holmann brought over an album and showed pictures of his three boys, aged 10, 11, and 12, who were in school at *Managua*. Marie and Johnny disappeared to the hotel where they ate dinner and stayed until the bar closed.

Johnny missed the train back to Rivas on Tuesday but left on the 6:00 a.m. train on Wednesday. On Thursday, everyone but Marie went on an excursion to *Peña Rota*, a secluded beach about a mile south of *San Juan* on land belonging to Mr. Holmann. Two horses had been sent over for Pic and Jan to ride; Jan's horse was red and a little skittish. The others drove by car as far as they could, then hiked through fields and gates, under fences, across several creeks, down a dry creek bed, ending up at a tree-shaded beach area literally alive with shells containing hermit crabs that inhabit loose shells. The girls showed up on their horses. They stripped to their bras and panties and all went into the water to fish----without much success. Persh caught a fish that looked like a rock, brown and covered with moss, with unusually colored fins, a colorful underbelly of white, cream, and pink, and a very huge mouth edged in yellow: it was a poisonous scorpion fish. On the way back to the car, Persh was sure he saw a deer and aimed, but Eileen yelled at him not to shoot just in time as it was a dog walking behind a man. After the girls had arrived back at the house, William and a boy came to take the horses back to the ranch. The boy rode the red one which threw him and ran away, but William was able to lasso it.

The girls got the horses again the next day and rode around town and along the beach to *Nacascolo* where they ran into Persh and Eileen. The waves were big and the surf was riled and dirty due to an incoming storm, so they all returned to the house where they found three visitors, two men from Wisconsin and one from Michigan who had just arrived. The Wisconsin boys were camping out on the lighthouse cliff. One was from Janesville, Charlie Montemayor, a geographer, and the other an artist from Milwaukee, Don Matting. The third fellow was John Steward from Dearborn, Michigan, an ex-Army officer who was going *"as far into South America as he could get"*. They didn't stay long but promised they would be at the train in the morning. That evening Marie and Persh were sick.

Saturday, July 31. Jan and Eileen went to meet the train which was late that morning because it had stopped to pick up two Americans, Charles Monet and William Wolcott, from Alliance, Ohio, and their Harley-Davidson motorcycles. They were coming down the tracks and Chuck had rolled over on a hill and hurt his arm. They both looked in fairly tough shape. The two fellows from Wisconsin were also at the station, and the girls took them to the house and gave them breakfast. The newcomers went to the

82

hotel to get cleaned up. Mr. Holmann came over and arranged for the Wisconsin boys to catch a launch for *Puerto Soley*, the nearest port in Costa Rica, at 2:00 p.m. They rushed off to get their belongings at their campsite, came back with their packs, took showers, and Persh took them to the dock to catch their launch. Marie and Eileen went to the beach for a while, then to the hotel for Cokes and found everybody there including the two new guys, Chuck and Bill. About 6:00 p.m. they all adjourned to the house; Mr. Holmann brought a pork roast for dinner. After dinner they played Liverpool rummy until Chuck and Bill left.

The Rivas family came to see them on Sunday bringing all sorts of good things with them. Most of the day was spent at the beach. The doctor brought two bottles of whiskey which was consumed during dinner. A mysteriously delivered package from Nelson arrived with a letter saying that he had given up trying to ride his bike to Panama, that he would sell it in *Puerto Arenas* or *San Jose*, Costa Rica, and travel to Panama by public transport. He sent his run-down bike battery for Persh to charge. That evening they received a wire from Charlie Montemayor asking Persh to find how much it would cost to get a boat to bring them back to *San Juan*. Apparently there was nothing at *Puerto Soley* but a house and a small airport and the only way out was by boat or small plane. Persh and Mr. Holmann went to see the man with the launch who said he would charge C\$60 (cordobas) and Persh could ride along. They also heard that a Peruvian boat, the *Santa Fe,* would charge \$125 per person and \$200 for each car. Bill and Chuck came to visit, and Chuck sketched a portrait of the monkey.

Persh left at 6:30 the next morning to catch the launch for the boys in Costa Rica. On the way back they fished and caught 14, including a big salmonette (red mullet) and a large fish called guyu. The Wisconsin boys camped in an extra room in the house, and Chuck and Bill came over for a delicious fish dinner after which they played rummy, poker, and black jack until 1:00 a.m.

The next couple of days were spent in fishing, swimming, and eating. There was quite a large group around the house with the American boys and the local fellows dropping in at all hours. As a special favor, Tobe made a batch of chocolate ice cream for the girls but there was barely enough for everyone to have a taste.

Thursday, August 5. The Wisconsin boys invited everyone to a barbecue at their campsite about a half mile away on the *El Faro* lighthouse cliff. Marie and Pic got up at 5:00 a.m., went to the butcher shop and selected a leg off a pig that was just being butchered. The boys, Don and Charlie, had ingeniously made a sheltered kitchen up there with a barbecue spit that had a seat around it, their jungle hammocks hung nearby. There was a magnificent view of the whole area: *San Juan* and the Bay, the ocean, and a beautiful sunset. While the pork leg was cooking, they sat around the campfire, sang songs, and told stories. Dinner was served at 10:00 p.m. followed by a rum party that broke up at 2:30 a.m. Johnny blew his top at the Ohio boys, told them they were snooty and had acted stuck up in *Managua* and were being friendly that night only because they wanted some good food. Bill and Chuck took it in good spirits. It might be noted, however, that when Chuck first met Eileen, he commented that he thought she was just *"another damned English-speaking native"*.

The next morning everybody came to the house, donned swim clothes, and went for a group swim. Johnny created a sensation by wearing Marie's striped bathing suit. Eileen took pictures. Some more Americans showed up in town----Larry White from California on his way to Panama, hoping to be back to California in time for school. He arrived just as Eileen was fixing her breakfast and looked so hungry she gave him her breakfast. Then he left to check into the hotel. At the beach they met two more Americans, a husband and wife, living in a house very near to them. They were in *San Juan* for a two-week vacation. He was a mining engineer from Texas working at India Mines in Nicaragua. The company was mining for gold which isn't usually associated with Nicaragua, but the country was a significant exporter of the precious metal.

On Saturday morning, Marie got up early and went to the train to get

Johnny. He wasn't on it, but Mr. Holmann, his wife, and young Carlos were. Marie was able to buy a good selection of fruits and vegetables including watermelon and cantaloupe for 1 peso each. Later in the day, Mr. Holmann came over and told them they should make the *Santa Fe* an offer. With their approval he wired an offer of $600 for both cars and six people. The house was the gathering point for all the travelers passing through----Chuck and Bill from Ohio, Larry from California, Charlie and Don from Wisconsin, John from Michigan. Don was a talented artist and promised Marie he would make a painting of the port for her when he got back to Milwaukee. Marie commented that *"despite all the fellows here, I miss Johnny very much. I wish I felt better---seems if it isn't diarrhea, it's indigestion, constipation, a cold, or the curse"*. She played a quick game of tennis with John from Michigan and commented on his athleticism: *"he has a wonderful build and is interested in all sports"*.

Sunday, August 8. Johnny was on the morning train, and Marie was there to meet him and shop for some produce. He was in a very cheerful mood and they were very happy to see each other. He had only been gone since Friday but she had *"really missed him terribly. It is so wonderful to be with somebody who you know really cares for you and you can talk to about anything. That closeness is something I miss"*. They returned to the house and ate breakfast. Later in the day Mr. Holmann came over and told them their ship was arriving so they all went over to sit on the porch of his office and watch the *Santa Fe* come in. It was originally a minesweeper that had been converted into a merchant ship used principally for transporting Peruvian lumber up and down the coast. Mr. Holmann had been told the ship would charge $800 for the cars and six people, coming down from their original price of $1150. After it docked, Persh and Pic had a long talk with the Captain at the hotel, and he agreed to take the Pickens party of seven with the two cars to Callao, Peru, for $700, leaving in two days (Tuesday). This included John Steward who had decided to travel to Santiago with the group. Marie and Johnny went to the hotel to hash over recent events. Knowing that Johnny had a strong jealous streak, she wanted to assure him that her activities with the American boys had not involved any romantic hanky-panky. Johnny was set to leave for the U.S. and planned to do so the week after the group left. Back at the house, farewells were said to Don and Chuck who left on the 4:30 p.m. train for Rivas. Everybody started packing up. At 8:00 p.m. Persh and John Steward went back to *Peña Rota* and returned at 2:30 a.m. with seven lobsters which Persh cooked before going to bed at 4:30 a.m.

Monday, August 9. The truck was out of commission; something was wrong with the gears. Persh worked on it all morning and Mr. Holmann brought his jeep over to pull the truck around but nothing worked. Chuck and Bill returned from Rivas saying they, as well as Larry from California, were leaving on another ship, the *Launchia*. Marie put Johnny in a difficult situation by asking him to go with her to get some soft water at Holmann's store. Johnny said that men never carried things such as jugs of water on the street---it was against their class traditions. Instead, he kept her company while she did some laundry, mending, and ironing. Mr. and Mrs. Holmann and young Carlos stopped by for a short visit. Marie and Johnny joined several of the group who went to the hotel for a few drinks. Marie had double whiskeys with ginger ale which went down smoothly, but when she and Johnny went to sit at the beach she became sick as a dog. Johnny was upset with her for drinking so much. Marie contended that it was the spicy sausage she ate for dinner that upset her stomach. They argued back and forth and by the time they returned to the house Johnny was feeling low and glum because their last night together had gone so poorly. He went to bed promptly and when Marie went to check on him *"he was taking it pretty hard, cried and everything, which didn't make me very happy either"*.

Tuesday, August 10. Mr. Holmann pulled the truck to the dock with his jeep and everyone else showed up at customs at 8:30 a.m. except John Steward who was a no-show. Marie and Jan went back to get him. A crowd of townspeople gathered to watch the vehicles being loaded onto the barge which then ferried them out to the ship. To lighten the load, everything was removed from the truck and it was loaded first-----with problems as usual. A sling made from ropes, braced with two boards at the top, was devised to lift and maneuver the truck. One of the boards split and went  flying into the air like a missile, landing near Mr. Holmann and right where Marie and Johnny had just been sitting. But the truck was successfully lowered onto the barge, and Persh and William went out to the ship with it. Loading the truck onto the ship from the barge took what seemed to be forever. At one point the truck was left dangling in mid-air for about 15 minutes with only a single strand of rope holding it. Loading the car was a much easier task, but it arrived on the barge with four dented fenders and, just as it was being set down, a board dropped down making a big dent in the roof. Meanwhile, Jan and Pic took the passports to Mr. Johnson, the Peruvian consul. At about that time Johnny proclaimed that he and Marie were married, but nobody took him too seriously as it appeared that it was a frantic effort to get Marie to stay. All but Persh ended up in Mr. Holmann's store where they were showered with cake, bread, cheese, sardines, juice, and colas. Mr. Holmann invited them to have coffee and pie with his mother and sister, took them on a tour of his house, and made a special sandwich to take to Persh. He then took them to the dock in his jeep. They loaded all their boxes and possessions onto the barge and were transported out to the ship where they walked up the gang plank and boarded the *Santa Fe,* accompanied by Johnny and Mr. Holmann. It was hard to say goodbye to Mr. Holmann. They tried to express their gratitude for all he had done for them. He wouldn't even let them pay for loading the cars and, of course, had been a perfect host and special friend, their councilor, protector, and guardian angel during their stay in *San Juan del Sur*. The Captain came out on the launch along with Mr. Kelly and Mr. Johnson, the Peruvian consul. The travelers paid the Captain their $600, John Steward paid his $100, and Kelly and Johnson returned to shore in the launch accompanied by a disconsolate Johnny Rivas.

Once on the ship, Marie wrote: *"The Santa Fe didn't look too bad----we had pretty nice cabins. I gave Johnny some letters to mail and some movie film for him to take to the States. He was terribly sad to see us go. We had changed his life so much since we pulled into Rivas that day in May and would surely leave a large vacuum in his life. But he adapts easily from one situation to another, so I believe he'll adapt quickly to life in the U.S. He'll either love it or hate it and it won't take him long to decide where he'd rather live and whether he'd like a Nicaraguan or an American girl for a wife. He'd marry me in a minute, but he isn't ready to be married as he has a long tedious career ahead as a doctor and is in no position to be tied down to a wife---even though she would be an exceptional one---ha! It wasn't long until I had to bid him good-bye and we shoved off. It wasn't long after that until I started feeling kind of sea sick".*

Marie didn't write in her journal again until the ship docked at Callao (Lima), Peru, on August 19.

The *Santa F*e at San Juan del Sur

**The last picture of Johnny
with Marie.
August 10, 1948**

88

Chapter 16: All at Sea

San Juan looked so beautiful when viewed from the sea, a peaceful port setting back in the Bay surrounded with high rocky cliffs on each side, backed by high, green hills with the sandy beach and sparkling blue water. They looked for someone on the beach to wave to but saw no one. Pic and Marie began to get seasick before the ship even cleared the Bay. Manuel, their attendant, showed them to their cabins and dinner was soon ready. They were served a hot drink and a strong "wine" that they later learned was pisco, the national drink of Peru. All retired early. John had a miserable seasick night in his hammock.

Everyone but Persh was seasick at some point during the voyage including Alfredo, the monkey. Marie and Pic suffered the most. The others generally lost several meals but felt fine before and after. The wildest day was Saturday, the 14th, when it was so rough that the dishes moved around on the table and the soup spilled.

On Thursday they were 600 miles off the coast of Colombia and the ship slowed from 10 knots per hour to 5 in order not to arrive in *Guayaquil* on Saturday night. The ocean depth at that point was 12,000 ft. Persh and John worked on the truck but to no avail. That night at sea was delightfully romantic with a bright moon and a soft tropical breeze, but on Friday it became stormy, rough, and cold. That day they crossed the Equator and had to set their clocks up an hour.

Guayaquil is the largest city in Ecuador and is located about 30 miles up the Guayas River which is navigable and flows into the Pacific Ocean at the Gulf of Guayaquil. The ship entered the Gulf about 3:00 p.m. on Saturday, proceeded up the channel, and docked at *Puná* about 8:00 p.m. *Puná* is a port town on the tip of a large island, *Isla Puná,* which lies in the middle of the Gulf and at the mouth of the river. The ship was immediately surrounded by canoes with people selling leather goods. Then came a launch loaded with customs men and other government officials. Some canoes carried alcohol that was loaded aboard. The travelers welcomed the calm of the channel; this was the first time everyone had felt good since they left *San Juan*. The night was very chilly and they found it puzzling that they were literally right on the Equator and it was so cold.

<u>Sunday, August 15.</u> The ship left *Puná* for *Guayaquil* at 8:00 a.m., sailing up the *Rio Guayas* which was very wide with marshy shores. Huts were built high on stilts along the shore for coping with floods and tides. There were also a lot of *langosta* (lobster) traps. They arrived at *Guayaquil* at noon. As seen from the deck, it was an attractive, interesting, and busy city, a stark contrast to *San Juan* that had been so peaceful and quiet. At first the passengers were not permitted to go ashore because the ship was due to leave at 5:00 p.m. Vendors came aboard selling  luggage, cigarette cases, bow and arrow sets, belts, and briefcases. Then the passengers were told they could go ashore from 3:00 to 5:30 p.m. They did so, found the post office and mailed letters but, it being Sunday, the stores were closed so they just walked the streets. Marie, Persh, and Eileen led the way. Store windows displayed some unusual things: Panama hats (which originated in Ecuador, not Panama), paintings, chess sets made of bone. They found a Safan drug store open and indulged in ice cream and other good stuff which really hit the spot after starving for such things in Nicaragua. Chocolate cake topped with chocolate ice cream cost US17¢. At 5:30 they returned to the dock and caught a launch back to the *Santa Fe* where they were welcomed back by the Captain. At this point they learned that Mr. Johnson, back in *San Juan*, had arranged for the *Santa Fe* to make a special trip south to Callao just for the Pickens group. In retrospect it seems probable that Mr. Holmann had also arranged to subsidize the fare for the group which would explain why the Captain so readily accepted their lowball offer of $600. Before leaving *Guayaquil*, they were able to observe the city and the harbor at night. The city was beautifully

illuminated, and the harbor was very busy with boats of all sizes and descriptions: excursion boats, banana boats, canoes, sailing ships bound for other countries, and also many sailboats emanating from the local yacht club. The *Santa Fe* said goodbye to *Guayaquil,* shoved off at 9:30 p.m., lumbered down the river to *Puná* where they dropped off the port Captain and customs men, and sailed out of the Gulf to the open sea.

The first stop in Peru was *Port Talara,* an oil center at the westernmost point in South America. Oil wells populated the barren hills along the shore and crude oil was pumped through pipelines to a refinery at *Talara.* It was a large port with many Americans. The *Santa Fe* tied up alongside the dock to take on oil, and the passengers were permitted to go ashore. A shopping center had several good stores with a lot of American things plus llama rugs and silver items. The market had great produce: tomatoes, cauliflower, and cabbage. At a bar, the girls met the Captain and three of his Navy friends, all commanders. Everyone adjourned back to the ship for refreshments in the dining room until the Navy men left in a launch to go back to their oil tanker. The travelers started arranging their things for customs, and the *Santa Fe* shoved off right after dinner.

The next day was cloudy, cold, and damp. Thousands of birds flew around the ship: gulls, pelicans, sea turkeys. The cars became caked with salt from the sea air. The passengers were told to be at lunch promptly at noon as the cook had a heavy workload that day. When the time came they discovered that Manuel had prepared a special lunch for Pic's birthday, August 17. He had concocted a mix of pisco and orangeade to drink before lunch and Burgundy wine with lunch. The radio operator brought a radio down to play some music for the occasion. Pic, who was always reluctant to reveal her age, turned 26 but wasn't feeling well enough to enjoy the event very much.

Chapter 17: Lima, Peru

<u>Thursday, August 19.</u> The *Santa Fe* anchored outside the harbor at Callao at 2:00 a.m. to await the Port Captain and wait for the fog to lift. When they docked at 7:00 a.m. a bevy of officials boarded requesting passports, titles, medical certificates, etc. The passengers said their goodbyes to the Captain, Manuel, and the others. The ship used a cleverly-engineered sling on the dock to unload the cars, an operation that went smooth and fast. From Callao, the *Santa Fe* would sail north to Panama and Venezuela. The travelers had been advised to keep a careful watch on everything on the dock as it was crowded with characters and thieves, particularly pickpockets. The truck had to be pulled to customs where the inspectors slammed and banged their things around, ripped the strings off parcels, then haphazardly slapped stickers on everything. They met two men who spoke English, one was from Janesville and the other was president of the Auto Club in Lima who took Persh into Lima to see if they could get a permit to admit the cars without paying duty. The others went uptown, got some money exchanged (14 sols per dollar), and had a pleasant lunch with Luis, a friend of the ship's captain. Persh returned with the news that the officials thought the import situation with the cars qualified as a carnet[16] which meant no duty but required some paperwork to be filled out and signed. Then a man told them it would cost 1,000 sol (US$71) for wharfage, but Luis was able to get it lowered to US$15. They were prevented from moving the cars without clearance, and the vehicles needed to be guarded so Persh and John stayed to work on the truck. The five girls tried to find a hotel in Callao but found nothing acceptable so took a cab into Lima. The ten-mile drive was over a beautiful wide road with a lot of open country and quite a lot of construction going on. Lima was a large city with wide streets, well lit, but the traffic was terrible, similar to Mexico City where everyone drives with their horns. They got two rooms at the *Hotel 28th de Julio*[17] which was quite an acceptable place, cleaned themselves up a bit, and ate at a corner restaurant

where they met Ed and Marsha, a cute couple from Berkeley, California. The movie theater next door was showing Tony Martin in "Casbah" in English with Spanish subtitles. Pic and Jan went to Callao the next morning to watch the cars while Persh and John came in to get something to eat and some tools; they had learned that the truck was a 1947 model, not 1948 as they had believed.

When Marie and Eileen returned to the hotel from shopping on Saturday, Persh and John were there. The truck was fixed and the vehicles had been cleared for 1040 sols (about US$75). To celebrate they all got dressed up, went downtown to the Trocadero Restaurant for dinner, then to the Central Theater to see "Berlin Express' with Merle Oberon.

On Sunday they were shown around Lima by Albert Morzan, a fellow the boys had met at the dock. He showed them some impressive homes, drove around the hills that were covered with crosses and monuments, and then to the beach which looked delightful, but cold, and finally took them to eat at Crema Rica, a cute place with good food in a downtown park.

On Monday, Persh and John took the cars to be washed, then they all gathered at the U.S. Embassy where they got their mail and met with the U.S. Consul who seemed cool and indifferent. Prices in Lima were quite cheap: gasoline--US6-9¢/gal; hotel room for two--US$1.80/night; wine--US35¢/fifth; taxi for 5 from Callao to Lima--US$1; a meal of steak and potatoes--US25¢. Temperatures were surprisingly chilly, averaging about 60°F, August being the coldest month in Peru.

They investigated the job situation in Lima as they had been running short on funds since their long stay in Nicaragua. On Tuesday they scouted American-owned companies: RKO, Wurlitzer, Coca-Cola, International Petroleum, Copper Corp, Chrysler, and some banks, all of which held nothing promising for any of them. After dinner, they checked out the *Gran Hotel Bolivar*[18] where John was staying. Then, looking for something to amuse them, they walked into the Embassy Club, a very upscale dinner club with a good orchestra and singer. The girls were immediately swamped with men, several of whom were Americans, two who worked for Goodrich and two Peruvians, one a millionaire who owned a local newspaper. Everyone danced a lot, and Persh and Babe got drunk. They stayed until the last dog home. Persh insisted he needed something to eat so he and John went off in quest of a restaurant but found none open so they went back to their hotels hungry. Marie said it was 4:40 a.m. by the time everybody got back to their rooms.

Eileen was the most employable of the lot since she had worked at an office job in Indianapolis. She had encouraging interviews with Panagra[19] at the airport and the Bank of New York. But on Thursday afternoon, Persh announced that they were leaving for Chile thanks to some financial assistance from John. Marie commented in her journal that she wondered if John would have the patience to put up with all the dilly-dallying and inefficiency of the group once they got on the road; up until now he had been with them only on the ship. The girls rushed to AAA for travel information and to the Chilean consul for visas. Persh took the vehicles for servicing and they all went to Callao to eat. They ended up at Luis's home where they met his wife and three kids. John talked Luis into reducing the unloading fees to $US20.

Friday was spent in preparation for the next leg of their journey; laundry, packing, and last-minute shopping. Jan, Marie and Babe each got a rug by bartering at the market. Persh and Eileen bought some small silver items, a rug, and some items made of llama fur.

Chapter 18: The Peruvian Andes

<u>Saturday, August 28.</u> Check-out time at the hotel was 2:00 p.m., and there was an argument in settling with the hotel over damage to the truck that occurred when a hotel chauffeur backed into it. The hotel took 50 sols off the bill and had someone hammer out the dents. A trip downtown was made to shop for food and gas and the animals were tied on, but it was 6:00 p.m. before they finally shoved off. The truck mileage was 7,652. Their stuff had become so disorganized on the ship that they didn't feel up to camping out, so 18 miles out of Lima they stopped at a small town up in the mountains and got four rooms in a pension for 30¢ each. It was a cool and pleasant stop. Persh and John played billiards until bedtime.

It was foggy next morning, but they soon climbed out of it once they got underway. They welcomed the sun when it finally broke through since they hadn't seen it for nearly two weeks. The mountains were barren grey rocks, but *Chosica,* the first town they came to, was very attractive. The land here was irrigated. The highway began to climb drastically, leading to an area where nitrate, copper, and other metals were being mined. The landscape now became ablaze with color. Not only were the buildings painted in bright colors, but the mountains themselves were every color imaginable---gold, green, orange, shades of blue. Hills of waste slag were grey and black. It seemed unbelievable that there could be so many colors in the mountains. Later they were driving through snow-capped peaks at an elevation of 14,529 ft. with ice and snow by the roadside and a glacier in the distance. The road followed the *Mantaro River* and ahead

there was a saw-toothed range of rocks standing alone. Each section was a different color and their colored reflections were cast onto the river. The sight was breathtaking. As they approached *San Mateo,* el. 10,330 ft.,

they began to see llamas with different colored ribbons on their ears along the roadside carrying wood. The road at these high elevations was challenging; mostly dirt or gravel, terribly dusty, winding, very narrow and treacherous

with no protection on the sides, rocks on the road, and cave-ins near the edges. A cable suspension bridge with a two-ton weight limit dropped, swayed, bounced, and rocked when the truck crossed it. A bus that approached right behind them stopped and all the people got off and walked across the bridge. They passed through the town of *Morococha,* elevation 14,900 ft., with its copper and silver mines. At these high elevations, they were susceptible to *soroche,* altitude sickness. They did not get sick but could not exert themselves without blacking out. Jan nearly passed out while driving when they were at a high elevation (above 14,000 ft.); Persh also experienced it when he jumped out and ran up a hill to take a picture. The road descended to 12,180 ft. into *La Oroya*, a very interesting, good-sized town that looked as if it had been chiseled out of a huge gray rock. *La Oroya* was the site of a very large metallurgical plant where copper, lead, and other metals were extracted from ore in a smelting process. There were many nice-looking villages on the mountainsides with fields laid out all the way to the top, outlined by irrigation ditches. The road passed through two tunnels as it slowly descended into a wide valley where they camped just outside *Jauja,* el. 11,200 ft., in a grove of trees. Despite a good dinner, a cold wind made sleep difficult and the llama rugs a necessity for warmth.

It was really cold when John woke them up at 5:30 a.m. but, by the time they ate breakfast and got going, it was noon and hot. At one point, a bridge across a river was so swaybacked they deemed it unsafe for the truck, so John gunned it across the river bed and climbed up the rocks on the other side; the car made it across on the bridge. They got gas in *Concepción* and had lunch in *Huancayo,* quite a large city, el. 10,690 ft.

They all enjoyed a delicious steak dinner which cost $US1.20 for seven people. When Marie set her plate aside, a woman rushed up and snatched all the food off it. After *Huancayo*, the road climbed higher and higher through stunning country, towering mountains all around, the land covered with field after field, each differently colored, outlined by stone fences. There were huts and small villages on the mountain-sides, green fields and trees around them. One village had cute little mud shacks with grass roofs. The mountains were so vast and the area so colorful that the travelers felt insignificant, overwhelmed by the splendor and dizzy from the

heights. Eileen's comment: *"The vastness and beauty seemed unreal, unlike anything I'd ever seen before and impossible to describe"*. Now the road descended rapidly around sharp, narrow hairpin curves. They had been hoping to find a river where they could camp and wash, but when one came into view they could find no access. Nevertheless they found a good place that was sheltered and had a nearby spring running down the mountainside where they could eat, bathe, and sleep.

Tuesday, August 31. It was another very cold morning. They packed and drove to *Mejorada* for gas and a quick breakfast. When they left and got to the edge of town, they were stopped by officers who told them that the road was under construction and traffic was one-way for the next 100 kilometers (62 miles) so they could not pass until the next day. A young man who spoke some English happened to be walking by and stopped to talk. Persh asked him if it was permissible to fish in the river. The man, who introduced himself as Henrique, invited them to his home at the edge of town. To reach the house, they had to cross over a stream on a rickety footbridge. Henrique made the visitors feel at home with a tour of his house that he had fixed up to be cute and cozy. He showed them his garden with calla lilies and elephant ears, his field of potatoes. He brought out albums of pictures, one of his sweetheart and one of his brother who got his naval training at Corpus Christi, Texas. He served them Coke and told them something about life in that area. He owned 400 llamas that roamed all around the place, also a large number of goats. The ribbons in the ears of the llamas and goats were because of Indian Fiesta. The Indians live on the mountainsides, own their own land, and speak their own language, *Quechua,* not Spanish. *Quechua* was the language of the Inca Empire. The travelers decided to camp across the stream from Henry's house. The three men went fishing but caught nothing. A mother goat got in the car and started eating the oranges. Late in the afternoon the girls dressed up and everyone went upstairs at Henry's house and danced to American records, talked, and drank *El Capitans*, a mixture of pisco and vermouth. Henry served a delicious dinner: lamb with soup, rice, potatoes, chicken and then apricots and coffee. Afterwards they all went back upstairs for more dancing and *El Capitans*. Henry had an Indian servant who was very bronze with black hair, a little chubby but very clean and smart looking. The girls wanted to take his picture but refrained from doing so out of respect for local customs. Henry showed them some spreads and blankets made by the Indians there at his house, noting that it took an Indian a month working six or eight hours a day to make one blanket. He gave Pic a doe skin. So what might have been a frustrating wasted day turned out to be very enjoyable, interesting, and educational,

Henry came over next morning with his beautiful red horse, visited while they were eating breakfast and stayed until they left. Jan took a picture of him and his horse with the house in the background. The countryside here was extremely dry with a lot of cactus. The road was smooth but very narrow with many sharp turns around boulders and other obstructions. They came into *Anco* hungry and thirsty but found no place to eat so continued on to *Huanta*. The  officer who stopped them on the edge of town asked to see their passports, then hopped on the truck and directed them to a pretty good restaurant on the Plaza. Seven large breakfasts with steak and French fries cost a total of $US1.29. The officer bought Eileen a pack of cigarettes and wouldn't take a peso. The roadside became somewhat greener as they progressed. Just as it was getting dark, they were sailing along on a curve when a tire on the truck went flat. A fellow who spoke English came along in a truck, offered to help and suggested that the girls might find a camping spot down the road a ways. While the men fixed the flat, the girls proceeded in the car and found a suitable spot near a stream where they could camp, clean up, and fix dinner. They were ten miles south of *Huanta* at an elevation of 8,000 ft. John had seemed quite moody all day, and after dinner he told them he intended to leave them as they weren't making good enough time. Marie was not surprised.

Thursday, September 2. The truck had another flat tire on the twenty mile drive to *Ayacucho*, a good-sized city, el. 9,000 ft. They attracted a huge crowd on the Square where the men fixed the tire. The ladies shopped around but didn't find anything to buy except some meat at the market. Kids, trying to be helpful and hoping for some money or a treat, flocked around and pressed against them so tight they could hardly move or breathe. Once out of *Ayacucho*, the highway began an extreme climb. The cars got hot and the radiators boiled. The water they found was so dirty they didn't want to put it in the radiators. They parked a little further up; Persh and Marie searched the area and found a stream where they got some better water. The climb continued into very barren country where there was no one but a few sheepherders tending huge flocks. A very big herd dog was mistaken for a predator. A shepherd walked toward them and waved, so they stopped to talk to him. He was dressed in typical shepherd garb and carried a very cute baby lamb, all white with a few black spots on its face. The shepherd also carried a ball of yarn and a spinning spool, so while he was walking and talking he was spinning away. He asked for a cigarette and they gave him half a pack and an orange. He was so happy to get the orange that he kissed it, but he was shy about having his picture taken and would not let them pet the lamb. There were many other shepherds along the way, mostly on foot but some were on horseback. It seemed that the road would never stop climbing but finally peaked at 13,800 ft. at *Tocto* Pass after which it began to descend. From the top they could see down for miles and miles with the road winding and turning in hairpin and horseshoe curves with a beautiful valley far below. They agreed it was the most magnificent view they had yet seen. They hoped to find a camping place where they could enjoy this scenic vista but had to descend further than they wanted to before finding a suitable place. It was full of cactus. John kicked it away, but all of them got thorns even thru the soles of their shoes. The spot was surrounded by huts made of adobe blocks with grass roofs and there were some all-grass huts.

They had to pick the cactus out of the tires next morning before they left. Even so, after just a short distance the truck had another flat tire which took three hours to fix. But it was in a level place with many huts around. The natives congregated around them. The women were very friendly; one asked if American houses were better than theirs. When Eileen gave them cigarettes, they were so happy they hugged and patted her, gave her some parched corn and a chunk of cheese and showed her how they did their spinning. The natives wanted the old tire: they would make shoes from it. The girls tried to barter with them to receive something in exchange for the tire, but the people were so poor they had nothing to offer,  although they did come up with two eggs. The kids were the worst looking ragamuffins and when Alfredo was let out of the car they flocked around him. To everyone's surprise, Alfredo seemed to enjoy having the kids pet him. A little girl had something wrong with her eye; her brother wanted to ride to the hospital in *Andohuaylas* to get medicine so they took him in the truck when they left. He didn't know how to open the car door and had a terrible scared look on his face during the whole trip. The road climbed up and up into godforsaken territory. A group of llamas displaying the color orange caught their attention; they later learned it was painted on them for identification. Alpacas also dotted the landscape in this area.

When they descended into *Andohuaylas*, el. 9,600 ft., and stopped for gas, Persh told them that the fourth tire was ready to blow. The little Indian said this was where he wanted to go but wouldn't leave the car. A big crowd gathered around. Marie finally figured out that the kid didn't know how to open the door so she helped him out and he left. They judged a restaurant that had been recommended to them to be too dirty, so they bought the makings for salmon sandwiches and took off. They climbed again and stopped to eat their sandwiches at a lovely high spot overlooking the town, fields, and animals below. The road continued to climb, taking them to an area that was very high, bare, wind-swept, and

cold. On the mountainside were big birds with curlicue beaks and some big white birds that Persh identified as snow geese. He tried to get close enough to shoot one but had no luck. As they were driving along, John tested to see how easy it was to pull the trigger on the gun. It was easier than he expected. The gun went off inside the truck and the bullet went through the floorboard between his feet. The noise inside was deafening and the cabin filled with gun smoke. Fortunately the bullet lodged in the floor and did not hit the motor. They found an interesting spot to camp down off the road near the stone foundations for an ancient Incan bridge that once spanned the *Apurimac River*. It was a perfect location, warm and relaxing.

The men took a bath in the river before they left next morning. The next town, *Abancay,* el. 7,800 ft., didn't have much to offer. The market didn't want to sell them anything but, after an argument, they were able to buy a little meat that turned out to be very tough. Their attempts to find a new tire or get one vulcanized to last until they got to Cuzco were futile. They were able to buy a piece of tire to use as a boot and learned that the old tire they gave away the day before was worth 50 sols. Eileen couldn't find her cigarette brand but found some Lucky Strikes; she was told it was illegal to have a lighter because the government had a monopoly on matches. Another big climb faced them when they left *Abancay* and they found themselves confronted with a most agonizing and bewildering sequence of extreme switchbacks and hairpin turns. Not too high up they saw a group of men dressed in suits on saddled horses lined up by the side of the road. They appeared to be paying tribute to a large red and white Peruvian flag flying on a hill across the road from them. After a long climb, the road began a rather rapid descent to 5,900 ft. into a valley where maguey was in bloom, the bloom resembling *"asparagus spears the size of telephone poles"*. They climbed again and entered an area where several landslides had occurred. Caterpillars and men with shovels were working to clear the roadway. The road now seemed to have transitioned from being a convenience for transport to being a major annoyance, as if there were a master  plan to impede their progress with a series of obstructions and flat tires.

At this point the travelers were about 25 miles due south of Machu Picchu as the crow flies, but there were no highway connections at that time. Two months later, in October, 1948, the *Carretera* Howard Bingham (Highway) to Machu Picchu would be opened. This was a six-mile road with 14 switchbacks leading to the ancient site from *Aguas Calientes*, a small town about 45 miles northwest of Cuzco.

After maneuvering through the landslide areas, another tire went flat on a windy curve, but the boys were prepared for it and had the boot ready to install. When they ran into another landslide area, they stopped for lunch, then descended again to the *Apurimac River* at 5,900 ft. It was dark when they stopped at a little hotel for some beers. The hotel was  out in the country, all alone and back from the road a bit. The bar was a dark, dimly lit room in the back of the building. There was no electricity so boys with flashlights escorted them in and out. Several men were eating dinner, and the smell of food made them so hungry they wanted to eat right then and there but decided they should save their money and eat the tough meat they had bought in *Abancay*. They called it rubber stew as it was very much like trying to eat a rubber band.

Sunday, September 5. They were on the road early, praying that the truck tire wouldn't blow out before they got to Cuzco. The road climbed a lot against a background of snow-capped mountains, then hit a pleasant flat plateau on which they could have made good time except for concerns about the truck tire. The girls stopped by the roadside for a "rest" but were interrupted when they looked up and saw a man approaching. Back on the highway, they passed through the small town of *Izcucacha*. They debated whether to stop there and eat but decided to drive on to Cuzco. The road climbed some more, then dropped down into a valley where they were rewarded with a bird's-eye view of the city. Across the way were some ruins, a cross, and a statue of Jesus Christ atop a hill. They had arrived in Cuzco, el. 11,440 ft., on that tire! Cuzco, the historic capital of the ancient Incan Empire. Vastly relieved, they went to Crema Rica for breakfast.

Chapter 19: Cuzco

After breakfast, they checked out the market which had a huge meat section and a good selection of vegetables. They were disappointed, however, in the limited variety of Peruvian specialties on display, being made up mostly of sleeveless sweaters, gloves and socks. The crowd consisted of a very interesting mass of people dressed in everything from Indian costumes to rags and tatters. The travelers were besieged by children begging for a *propina* (a tip of money). Outside the market all sorts of food was being sold to throngs of people huddled around in circles eating it. The smell was nearly overpowering from lack of sanitation with children going to the toilet anywhere. Persh was hounded by a man from a local newspaper wanting their names and addresses. They found John uptown talking to Mr. Michael Sumar and his five cousins, all quite good looking fellows. Michael owned a clothing store. He showed them around to several prospective camping grounds, one in a park, one on a baseball diamond, and one in a field where they chased llamas down the road. They chose another one in a riverbed near a house Mr. Sumar was having built, mainly because running water was available from the construction site. After cleaning up a bit, they asked a policeman to direct them to a nearby ruin, *La Fortaleza del (The Fortress of) Sacsayhuaman*, famous for its walls made of huge stones shaped to a perfect fit with one another. As with every other visitor, they had to marvel at *"how they got those stones, tremendous in size, stacked on top of each other"*. From the Fort, dating back to the year 1100 and located 700 ft. above the city, there was a great view of the city below. Next they went to the museum, *Museo Inko* that traced Cuzco's history from the Inca period to the modern era. It was closed on Sundays but they learned that Cuzco was a *Quechua* word meaning "navel" to designate it as the center of the Incan empire. They ran into Michael Sumar again in a souvenir shop that featured Indian costumes. He recommended *Salon De Tea, Buenos Aires* as a good place to eat. The food wasn't very good, but the bill was only 19 sols so they didn't complain. They debated whether to go see Alan Ladd in "Saigon" but the next showing wasn't until 9:30 so they decided to go to bed. Persh and John, however, walked downtown, drank wine and pisco all evening and spent only 16¢ because everyone wanted to buy them drinks. People got into arguments over who would buy the next round. The newspaper apparently had given them some good publicity.

The boys went to town the next morning to shop for tires. They learned that their size #717s were not made nor used there, so they were extremely lucky to find two perfect tires of the right size for $25. Pic and Jan took their trinkets to the market to see if they could barter for something but didn't have much luck. The day was spent mostly in getting settled and stocking up on necessities. Mr. Sumar invited them to a Serenade at midnight for his brother's birthday, but they declined because it was an outdoor event and they were cold. But at 3:00 a.m., they were awakened by the Serenade that had come to them. It consisted of Mr. Sumar and three Indians full of pisco. They sang several songs, some in *Quechua*, then left. The girls enjoyed it as they were tucked warmly in bed.

The tires were changed around first thing the next morning. Pic and Jan picked up Michael Sumar and they all went sightseeing. First they went back to *Sacsayhuaman* but at a higher level where there were places of worship and relics of everyday living such as bathtubs. There was an outside playground area that had a slide area. A little boy demonstrated by sliding down on his stomach on a goat skin, then gave the skin to Persh to try. He went down on his seat, landed hard on his feet with the impact throwing him up in the air. They were next taken through a tunnel that was very dark and so low they had to bend over and hang on to each other's coattails. From there they climbed high to a second level, then higher still to a third level which was the most impressive; huge blocks of stone laid in rows so straight they formed a channel for running water that still ran through it. Michael told them about a big tunnel said to exist beneath Cuzco. Several men were reported to have entered to explore it but never returned. Michael, Persh, and John became excited about getting up an expedition from the States to investigate this subterranean passage.

Michael told them he had gone on several archaeological expeditions with Dr. J. H. Rowe, an American archaeologist and anthropologist well known for his extensive research on the Inca civilization in Peru. Michael also told them something about his personal history: that as a wild child he left home at an early age, went into the jungle where he panned for gold, found enough to start his clothing store; that he owned two farms, one of 100 km² (38.6 sq. miles), the largest in the Cuzco area on which he was raising llamas, vicunas, alpacas, and goats; that he also owned a tin mine and one other mine. This information was taken with a grain of salt as they detected in Michael a tendency to embellish his status. Later they learned that his story was probably true. He told them that when they got to Santiago they should look up his cousins at the Sumar factory where raw cotton from the States was ginned and spun into cotton fabric.

After a late lunch, they visited the Cathedral on the Plaza. Construction was begun in 1559 and completed 100 years later. Many of the stones used in its construction were taken from *The Fortress of Sacsayhuaman*. The interior was very impressive with many paintings, icons, gold statues, and wood carvings. Just inside, in a gold frame, hung a huge painting of The Last Supper which showed the meal being served to be a guinea pig. This was not as odd as it seemed since guinea pig (*cuy*) is a delicacy in Peru. The main altar, aptly called the silver altar because it was covered in a ton of silver, was topped by a statue of Our Lady of the Assumption to whom the cathedral is dedicated. From the Cathedral they went to *Qoricancha, Templo del Sol* (Temple of the Sun) where the highest Incan priests once lived. The building was originally lined with gold, the walls were gold-plated, the rooms and hallways contained thousands of gold statues and idols. At its central point was a gigantic golden disk which reflected the sun into the courtyard. Though the gold was gone, the sun still shone on this disk and during the summer solstice was said to reflect the light onto the seat of the highest priest. Gold was not valued by the Incas because it was rare or precious but because gold was the closest thing on earth to the brilliance of the sun. Spanish reports said the opulence of *Qoricancha* was *"fabulous beyond belief"*. The Spaniards, of course, looted all the gold, desecrated the temple, and built a Catholic Cathedral on top of it. The travelers were shown through the temple by a priest and a small boy; their main recollection was of some very old paintings on the walls. Michael invited them to see his collection of paintings. They were located in two rooms above his clothing store. Like something one could imagine in a mystery story, they entered through a dark stone hall, then up stone steps, through a rickety door, and down a spooky looking hallway. The "living room" was small and cluttered with old books, trinkets, and paintings that were ripped, faded, and cracked, some supposedly dating back to the Inca period. The "bedroom" had an unmade bed, the walls were papered with paintings and there was not a square inch that wasn't covered with some object, everything under a thick layer of dust. Michael was also a writer and gave Babe one of his books, a small one with short stories in Spanish, all dedicated to some person. He gave them some old Spanish coins as souvenirs when they left.

Chapter 20: Lake Titicaca and on to Chile

<u>Wednesday, September 8.</u> They were up early and went into town for some final shopping. Marie and Jan traded for suede purses, Persh got a canoe. John went to Sumar's store, bought a poncho, and got some money changed. When they left Cuzco at 2:00 p.m., the truck mileage was 8,417. The road here seemed passive, oblivious to their presence as it took them on a flat plain surrounded by mountains. The area was quite heavily populated with friendly people wearing colorful clothing who waved and smiled at them; there were also many dogs that loved to chase the cars. Most of the Indian women wore men's felt hats, long heavy skirts in gay colors, and shawls. Some wore shoes but many went barefoot. The travelers were captivated by the magnificent ponchos that the natives were wearing and tried to buy one from an old man and his brother but they refused to sell. The men spoke *Quechua* only and beamed when they were given a couple of cigarettes. A campground was found just south of *Sicuani* near an irrigation ditch and some trees that had a peculiar odor. John had an attack of the chills.

They arrived in *Ayaviri*, el. 11,800 ft., about 11 a.m. next morning, just in time for a big festival coming from the church. There was a parade with clowns, Indian war dancers and costumed girls dancing with them, men in costumes, followed by a band with a religious float all in white featuring an exquisite doll, then a priest in front of several men carrying a baby. At each corner of the plaza were very tall booths displaying religious articles. The priest stopped at each booth, burned incense, gave a blessing, and passed on to the next booth. It was like a Hollywood production. The Indian dancers were outstanding, very well-choreographed and costumed, their dance steps tuned to the mood of the occasion. The group felt fortunate to have witnessed the event and took quite a few pictures. Their visit to the market came up with nothing, so they hit the road for *Pucara* arriving there at siesta time. The town was dead, but they were directed to a pottery place behind a high mud fence where everyone but John traded for small pottery pieces: ashtrays, birds, bulls, and Indian heads. Eileen traded an old blue T-shirt for two vases, the Peruvian national bird[20], and a head. From there they hurried on to *Juliaca* and found a store where llama rugs were being sold by a woman who was very cordial and gave them some vermouth to drink. Babe traded a gold pearl necklace for a big llama rug and a small throw rug. They found a camping spot at the edge of town. At an elevation of 12,550 ft., the night was so cold that John and Marie slept in the truck with Persh and Eileen which made for an uncomfortable night. Ordinarily John slept in his sleeping bag outside or in his hammock when the weather permitted.

Juliaca was a jumping-off spot for Lake Titicaca and a trading center for woolen goods and skins. Since the travelers were so low on funds, they concentrated on bartering for local goods. Some people came to their camp next morning to do some trading. Eileen had brought along a good supply of cast-off clothing which went over well. One man was very interested in a white shirt that Eileen presented for barter. He handled and examined it several times and offered six pairs of socks in trade, but she held out and eventually managed to get seven pairs. A woman wanted to trade a beautiful rug for Marie's raincoat. A store that had excellent rugs wouldn't trade for jewelry and knick-knacks, but gave up a white rug for four shirts and an old sports coat. Another rug was traded for two dresses, a housecoat, flannel pajamas, and a deck of cards. John, Persh, and Eileen drove the truck on to *Puno*, leaving the girls behind to shop. *Puno,* el. 12,550 ft., stands right on the shore of Lake Titicaca, the worlds' highest navigable body of water. It straddles the border between Peru and Bolivia. It was late before the girls caught up with them because they had car trouble when leaving *Juliaca* and had to call a mechanic for help. Together again, they all did more trading at a rug store. It was so cold they decided to eat out, found a pension that offered dinner for 7 sols which they thought was too much and haggled the price down to 4 sols. Only after being led through a horrible looking bedroom, through a kitchen and up some rickety old stairs did they realize that the price included room and meals. Dinner by itself was only 3 sols and was edible, but Marie was unable to keep hers down. They found a place to park at the edge of town where they spent another cold night. They didn't realize until next morning that their campground was at the city jail.

There was more trading for rugs in *Puno* the next morning. Once again Eileen proved to be the master trader by getting two matching throw rugs for a red two-piece dress, two short-sleeved sweaters, and a pair of long johns. Marie was peeved that the others had brought so much old clothing for barter. She had been warned about how little space they would have so she brought only good clothing that she expected to need. Furthermore, she had given Pic and Jan several articles of clothing before they left Wisconsin because *"I thought they needed them worse than I did"*. Now it galled her to see those garments being traded away to the Indians. Still, she admitted, *"I did manage to dig out enough things that the Indians like so that I've gotten quite a lot of nice things for myself"*.

It was 2:30 p.m. by the time they made sandwiches, got gas, and left town. The road was flat and ran along the lakeshore for a distance on the way to *Llave*. There they encountered a wedding parade; women wearing skirts of many different colors were dancing on the square. The highway they had been taking led straight into Bolivia 50 miles ahead, so they turned south toward the coast. It soon became dark and very cold as they were at an elevation near 13,000 ft. They continued driving in hopes that the road would descend into a warmer elevation, but by 9 p.m. they started to look for a place to stop. Two men flagged them down and warned them about a bridge ahead. When they got to the bridge, the road was blocked with rocks and a fellow told them they would have to wait until morning to cross. But they were actually being held up by con-men as they were then told that for 10 sols the rocks would be removed and they could cross. John, who was driving the truck, said he'd pay 5 sols only. The men agreed and removed the rocks, permitting them to cross over what was quite a long bridge and eventually find a camping spot out on the very cold desert floor. They went to bed without eating, covered themselves with llama rugs and spent a miserable night.

Sunday, September 12. John got up early and built a fire out of some

110

brush. By the time they ate, the sun was out and it was quite warm. The road was flat but soon began to climb and climb some more. The car stalled on a switchback; the carburetor was acting up. Eventually the uphill highway took them into very stark country with big clumps of grass, moss-covered boulders, and pin-cushion cactus. Vicunas appeared to be grazing on nothing but sand. Then, many miles away and far beneath them they began to see the terraces that had been laid out hundreds of years before, all banked with rocks, very green with many types of animals grazing on them. Every little piece of land was terraced. As seen from high above, it looked like a stunning piece of art. Eventually the road descended into *Tarata*, el. 10,690 ft., a very clean old town tracing its origins back to the year 450, pre-dating even the Incas. The cars were very low on gas and, after driving around, they found a store that had gas in barrels for US15¢ a gallon. A young boy persuaded them to eat at a pension. The food was very good and they truly pigged out, starting with pork, beef, and chicken, with spaghetti and a good sauce followed by steak, eggs, and potatoes with a delicious bread. They drank 22 cups of tea and coffee, Persh had seconds on nearly everything, and the total bill was $US1.50. As they left town on a very narrow street, they had to contend with people driving their livestock in from pasture. Just before dark, the road took them down a very steep hill with hairpin curves so sharp they had to back the cars up and make second tries. For miles the road condition was terrible and very narrow as it climbed further and further up. After a while it alternated between climbing and descending and eventually descended to an area that was very dusty and dry. The air became calmer and warmer as the road dropped down to the desert where they ran into fog. They drove in fog along the desert floor for quite a ways. As they neared *Tacna,* they decided to camp in the shelter of a huge signboard which provided some protection from the wind and mist. They enjoyed their meal of soup and sand amidst a huge feeling of relief not to be freezing in the night.

On Monday morning they drove on into *Tacna*, el. 1810 ft. and 22 miles north of the Chilean border. They found the Chevrolet agency whose owner, Mr. Canape, was very cordial but spoke no English. He called in Elisa, a very cute and delightful girl, to translate. Then Max Castillano came in and took over. He supervised the servicing and repair of the vehicles, then took them to the passport office and called the aduana who came at once to the Chevrolet office. Elisa recommended Martins as a place to eat and sent a boy to show the way; it was a pension but the food was not much to their liking---too spicy and too pricey. They found a jewelry shop owner who was willing to trade, so Pic, Babe, and Marie swung into action, ending up with some marvelous silver items including bracelets, wristwatch bands, cufflinks, tie-tacks, pins, and brooches. When the vehicles were ready, Max and Elisa accompanied them to customs at the edge of town. The office was closed, but Max got them to open, told them the travelers had nothing to declare, only clothes and baggage. The inspector flashed a light around on things in the car and truck and raised the gate. Goodbyes were said to Max and Elisa who were thanked for their helpfulness and kindness. After driving about 19 miles through flat desert of solid sand, they arrived at the Peruvian customs stop where they showed their papers, got some water, and found a camping spot nearby on a road leading to a big house. Just as they were preparing to eat their stew, two men from customs came. Someone had reported that they were trying to escape paying import duty on the cars, but the matter was soon resolved since the cars were not being imported into Peru but only passing through for which they had been issued a carnet when they arrived in Callao. Everybody was fatigued and very sleepy due to the changes in temperature and altitude; the heights had really affected them. They all hopped into bed as soon as they ate and enjoyed a good night's sleep on what they thought would be their last night in Peru.

Chapter 21: Trouble at the Border

<u>Tuesday, September 14.</u> When they awoke there was no doubt they were in the desert; nothing but sand as far as the eye could see. The parrot got under the car and came out only after much time-consuming cajoling. They arrived at Chilean customs about 8:30 a.m. There the cars and tires were checked and a police officer rode into *Arica*[21] with them. They had to pay for some forms at an office, then they were informed that the cars had to be bonded to bring them into Chile. Since the intent was to sell the cars in Chile, they were considered imports and had to be covered with an import customs bond to guarantee the payment of import duties and taxes. This threw them for a major loop for which they were completely unprepared. The only course of action they could think of was to see if Mr. Canape at *Tacna* could help them. He also owned the *Arica* Chevrolet agency, so they went there to ask for assistance. Mr. Canape, of course, was in *Tacna;* George Koch was the manager at *Arica* and he refused to even consider issuing a bond for them. He impressed the group as being "*a snot and an American, too*". When they returned to the customs office, the cars were impounded and could not be moved until the matter was settled. It was noon and siesta time so nothing could be done until after 3:00 p.m. They looked for a place to eat and stumbled across a hall that led past a kitchen to a courtyard full of birds. In the courtyard was a dance floor and a dining area that had little bamboo huts over the tables. They enjoyed a very fine and filling dinner with wine for US$2 for all. Pic and Jan called Max who said to meet him in *Tacna* at 5:00 p.m., but the Chilean authorities wouldn't let them leave. Pic argued with an officer who kept saying "*Mañana. No traffic after 5:00*'" but finally relented and sent a soldier with them to the border. They were now officially a group of people without a country as they were without visas or permits for either country. They proceeded back to *Tacna,* slipped through the police post and through customs at the edge of town, then went to Elisa's home to search for Max and found him eating dinner at an Italian restaurant. Elisa called an officer in the Peruvian

Army to help get them legal at the police station because they had come into town without reporting, but the police kept their passports. A conference was convened at Elisa's house to discuss their situation. The folks at *Tacna* Chevrolet were familiar with this procedure as they occasionally shipped autos into Chile. Several possibilities were presented and considered, and it was finally mutually agreed that *Tacna* Chevrolet would loan them the money for a bond for the two vehicles and hold the car for guarantee until the loan could be repaid. It was understood that they would have to remain in *Tacna* until the bond was issued and signed. A very weary and discouraged group of travelers camped for the night in a field at the edge of town. The truck mileage was 9,008.

They took their time getting up next morning, using the water from an irrigation ditch to clean themselves up a bit. A large group of cavalry came out to the field for maneuvers and an officer came over to talk to them. A civilian character who came strolling by offered to buy the car for 15,000 sols (about US$1000). They gathered again at Elisa's, got their passports back from the police station, visited the aduana's office, and shopped for food at the market. After lunch Marie and Eileen stayed with the truck while the others took the car to the Chevrolet office to see Max and Babe who was staying there because she was sick (small wonder!). Later, back at the camp, three fellows came by. One of them, Ed Perez, spoke some English and offered them a better place to camp at the water plant on the other side of town where he worked as a supervisor. They moved there promptly and found an enclosed area landscaped with lovely flowers, with running water and a room they could use. Elisa came with them and stayed for dinner after bringing wood so they could build a very welcome fire.

Ed came by the next day and brought sardines, tuna, and four bottles of wine. He took Persh and John to the city club to play ping-pong. Persh beat the *Tacna* city champ.

On Friday, Ed came again, this time with his cute wife, Amelia, and brought honey, eggs, head lettuce, and wine. Persh sold his big saw to Max for 90 sols. In the late afternoon Elisa came with her father and mother and brought ice cream. Persh and John got into an argument about how to build a fire, but after the fire was started everyone sat around it and talked.

<u>Saturday, September 18.</u> An early morning trip to the market was necessary as Ed and Amelia were invited to dinner; twelve mouthwatering T-bone steaks were purchased for US70¢. At mid-morning Marie, John, Persh, and Eileen went to *Agua Caliente* about 15 miles east to take a bath in naturally occurring warm water which ran through a sunken cement tub almost big enough to swim in. It was so relaxing they were reluctant to leave. On the way back, they stopped at a hotel in *Pachia* to have a Coke. That led to *pisco*, that powerful drink made from distilled wine. Persh dared Marie to down three in a row which she did. She had a glow on her face when they left the hotel. When they arrived at the Chevy office back at *Tacna,* she threw up several times. Elisa took her to the restroom and the mother gave her a family remedy for an upset stomach, never being told what the real problem was. Eileen volunteered that it must have been the warm water bath. Elisa agreed, saying that she had once been sick after a bath there too. When they got back to camp, Ed and his wife were there. Marie remained knocked-out in the back seat of the car. The guests were told that she had gone out to dinner with two pilots they had met at the hotel. Ed told them local color stories about the Indians living on corn and how they use cocaina (cocaine) for energy, about the monument atop the hill that commemorates the Battle of Alliance Heights (Batalla del Alto de la Alianza) in which Chile defeated a Peru-Bolivian army in 1880. (*Tacna* remained under Chilean control until 1929). Before the guests arrived, a dog had gotten the meat off the table and dragged it through the sand but had been stopped before he'd eaten any of it. The girls had washed the meat a couple of times to get the sand out, and Eileen gave it a third going-over until it was so pale it looked nothing like a T-bone steak. Still it didn't taste too bad although Eileen thought she could detect the taste of sand in it and hoped the guests would think it was salt. After dinner they sang songs around the fire. Ed and Amelia had splendid voices and sang some songs in Spanish for them.

On Sunday, the Perez family held a cocktail party in their honor at noon at the Union Club. Three different cocktails were served: martinis, a Tom Collins made with pisco, and a chocolate-flavored drink made from a native bush. When they returned to camp, Max came over with his wife, Jenny, who was a physical education instructor. After they left, the group was invited to Elisa's house for tea which developed into a dinner with turkey, ham, cheese, and sweets. After dinner, Elisa played records of Spanish music and showed them how to dance the Raspa, a folk-dance; also the tango and a Quechua dance that involved waving a handkerchief and was *"something like a rooster chasing a hen around"*.

Persh didn't feel well on Monday morning. At 8:30 a.m. he took John to catch the train to *Arica* where he would catch a plane to Santiago and meet them there. John left reluctantly and only because there was no room for him as they traveled south to Santiago with everybody packed in the truck. He had to leave his rug behind because he learned that permission was needed to take it out of Peru, so the girls rushed into town to seek permission for their rugs. In the meantime the travelers were expecting to hear at any time that their bond had been issued and they were free to go. Ed and his wife came to say goodbye but no word. In the evening they went back to Elisa's. She and her brother took them to the movie theater where they saw three shows for US5¢.

Elisa called at 9:00 the next morning saying the papers would be ready for signature that afternoon. At 2:00 p.m., Max and Elisa accompanied Persh and Eileen to the lawyer's office, then to the aduana to get the contract for the bond signed. The aduana was a funny little guy who wore very thick glasses, hovered over the typewriter, and wrote ninety miles an hour on it. Max made out the contract for *Tacna* Chevy to hold the car. Persh secretly hoped that they would offer to buy it for 25,000 sols and pay the import duty on it, but that didn't happen. After dinner, the girls spent the evening at Elisa's house. Back at camp everyone prepared for departure the next day.

Mr. Canape, Marie, Max, Jan, John, Pic
Elisa in front

Chapter 22: Tackling the Atacama Desert

<u>Wednesday, September 22.</u> It was noon by the time they were ready to leave. Elisa, Max, and Mr. Canape went with them to the police, the local aduana, and Pare Control outside of town. There was a sorrowful parting from these fantastic people who had been so kind to them and who seemed genuinely sad to see them leave. Everyone was curious to see what the seating arrangement would be. They packed themselves in, four in front and two in back, and took off. The police stop was routine but the man at the aduana station wanted papers for the rugs which, fortunately, the girls had obtained. They argued with him when he wanted to examine everything in the truck so he agreed to check only a few suitcases. Across the border into Chile, the customs stop in *Chacalutta* sent a soldier to escort them to the police in *Arica*. There they had to fill out some more papers and deliver them to George Koch at *Arica* Chevy who became angry because one of the forms was filled out improperly. A ballpark just outside town served as a camping spot, but in positioning the truck to find shelter against the wind it became stuck in sand. The night was too cold and dark to work at freeing it so they had dinner and settled in. Marie slept in the front seat, Pic and Jan in the back of the truck, Babe on boxes behind the front seat, Persh and Eileen together in a sleeping bag. Santiago was 1,060 miles away.

They awoke next morning to find a vulture watching them. They shooed it away as it came quite close making them wonder whether it was after them as well as their garbage. In an effort to get the truck out of the sand, they borrowed some boards from a neighbor who came to help. Just then a truckload of men drove by and stopped to help push it out. Freed from the sand, they drove into town and checked in with George Koch, customs, the police, and the market, and were finally free to go and underway by 1:30 p.m. The highway climbed very steeply and the truck stalled on the steepest grade. The road was very rough and curvy and progress was slow because of the heavy load. Twenty-two miles out of *Arica*, a big puddle of oil spurted up through the gear shift and all over their shoes. It was too far to the next town that had a garage, so they went back to the Chevy place in *Arica* where the mechanic found that he had packed the gear box full of grease instead of half-full, so he remedied it by taking some out. Now they retraced their steps through this inhospitable, desolate landscape. Further on they came to a customs stop in a green valley. Two men came out, had Persh take the animals off, flashed their lights around the truck, and sent them on. They camped high on a hill at the side of the road on a little curve. The presence there of an enormous brush pile was a mystery as there was no plant life living nor dead within miles, but it provided shelter and wood to make a fine bonfire. There was quite a bit of traffic on the road at night including cows and horses being driven to who knew where.

It took three hours for everyone to get ready the next morning. While loading up, they noticed a hubcap was missing. After back-tracking eight miles, it was miraculously found by the roadside. They dropped down to a creek where they stopped, got water in the cans, filled the radiator, and everyone took a bath as the water was quite warm. The next town, *Zapiga*, looked as if it had been destroyed by some natural disaster. At customs they were told it had once been a booming mining town for nitrate fertilizer with 20,000 people, but the mine had been closed for twenty years due to lack of demand. When they asked if they could get something cold to drink, an officer brought them bottled papaya juice. The customs officers were amused by how tightly packed the passengers were in the truck. The passengers, in turn, had adopted a know-nothing policy: just sit tight and pretend to know little Spanish (no great pretense required). This pose saved a lot of hassle as requests from officials who wanted to search their belongings were pleasantly and politely ignored. As they left *Zapiga* they could see how the land was dug up like mole hills where the miners had dug for nitrate and never leveled it off. Their attention was attracted to a very unusual huge cemetery with hundreds of crosses out in the middle of the barren desert. Each grave had a cross with a mound of dirt the size of a bed, some actually had bed frames around them. Some mounds were formed over large gas cans, some had hoods or other forms of protection against the severe weather at the head of the mound. Dates on the gravestones ranged from 1900 to 1946. It was dark and bitter cold when they arrived at *Huara* where they stopped for gas and meat, then decided to drive to *Iquique* to camp, assuming it would be warmer since it was on the coast. At *Humberstone,* site of a huge nitrate mine that was brightly lit at night, a truck driver said to follow him as he was driving to *Iquique.* The road was rough, curvy and mountainous, and it became foggy as it descended from a very steep mountain into the city which was a hub for nitrate and iodine production. Water had to be piped in from sixty miles away. There were horse-drawn surreys with chauffeurs dressed in black on the well-lighted streets. Because of the heavy mist, they settled on a cheap hotel instead of camping: the *Gran Hotel-Español* charged 80 pesos for one room with two beds. That included a savory dinner, but the beds were soft and the room was stuffy. Pic and Jan slept in the truck. Mileage on the truck was 9,350. Santiago: 985 miles away.

They intended to cook breakfast out of town next morning, but the hotel served bread, butter, and *coffee con leche* which appeared to be the typical breakfast in Chile. The Ford garage that was recommended to them didn't have the right oil for an oil change, and Persh had to flush out the transmission box himself. At the market they met Dave White, an American Methodist minister, who took them to his home where they met his wife and children. While they were eating ice cream, Mr. and Mrs. Wade, teachers at the Methodist school, came over and invited them to their place for lemonade. When they finally left *Iquique* at 2:30 p.m., they had to climb the steep mountain of sand that they had descended the previous night. From the top there was an amazing view of the city below, the ocean, and one huge sand hill on which the wind created a sandstorm worthy of the Sahara Desert. They rejoined the highway at *Humberstone* and drove south on a decent road through more nitrate mining country. The road ran straight as an arrow but they did not feel at ease on it. It was a long distance between towns and the mid-day heat was insufferable. Jan summarized their trip through the Atacama: *"blistering heat all day, freezing cold at night"*. The strong wind blew Lorito's cage off the truck twice and sent it tumbling and flying down the road in pieces. Each time they expected the parrot to be dead but she remained on her own two feet, hobbling along and screeching her displeasure as they retrieved her. They camped on the desert amid a cold, howling wind.

<u>Sunday, September 26.</u> They stopped at *Maria Elena*, site of a large nitrate mining company, partly U.S.-owned, and wanted to see the mine. A guard took them to the club where they were served orange and papaya juice and beer. When they asked for water they were referred to Mr. Christiansen, a Danish man, who served them sandwiches and more beer in his office. He had been in Chile for 30 years but at the mine for only a few months and had a family in Santiago. He went with them to the plaza and bought them ice cream and cake. They changed a few dollars into pesos and when they returned to the truck, Alfredo had locked the doors from the inside. Persh took a long wire from Lorito's cage and was able to jimmy the lock open. The road was a terrible washboard for several miles but later turned into good asphalt, but very narrow, built up on both sides with sand; to pass someone it was necessary to go off the road and drive through the sand. Along the way they passed many nitrate mines, and alongside the roadway they observed what looked like children's playhouses decorated with crosses and wreaths which they were told marked spots where someone had been killed. They hoped to bypass *Antofagasta* but learned that there was no bypass. They were able to make good time for quite a ways and camped 20 miles outside *Antofagasta* near a railroad station. A cold, bitter wind came up and blew in a thick fog which seeped through every crack and crevice. Santiago: 695 miles away.

They were unimpressed by *Antofagasta* when they drove into it next morning; the largest city in northern Chile and a big seaport. The area was known for its copper production. The market was disappointing so they settled for some beef and oranges, got some water for the radiator and were on their way. The road took them up some hills, then straight down into valleys several miles wide. While Persh was sleeping, they took a wrong turn onto a godforsaken, desolate road that was narrow, bumpy and full of pot-holes. It led them to Catalina which was nothing more than a dot on the map. Driving In the dark they were confused by a maze of roads, so when they came to an old abandoned fort with high walls, they backed the truck to a door, unloaded, and cooked inside.

When they rejoined the highway next morning, the road was rough and narrow but flat. At *Pueblo Hundido,* a gold-mining town, they bought some popina, a local fruit, and got air in the tires, then continued on to *Inca de Oro*, another gold-mining town that was quite picturesque. The gas cap was missing when they stopped for gas at a Chinese station, but the highway continued to improve and everyone was very helpful. They camped just beside a railroad bridge behind a rock pile about 20 miles north of *Copiapo*. It wasn't so cold that night. Santiago: 443 miles away.

The next morning they drove into *Copiapo,* a pleasant modern town with trees and flowers that were a very welcome sight after hundreds of miles of the Atacama Desert. At the bank, Persh met Mr. Holland from Santa Rosa, California, who went to the market with them and bought them oranges. They stocked up on grocery staples, treated themselves to ice cream at an American-style parlor, got air in the tires, sent a telegram to John in Santiago, and departed. The highway here had a wide roadbed but the road itself was very rough. They played Twenty Questions to pass the time. Eventually the highway dropped down into a green valley to *Vallenar,* another good-looking, clean town with many beautiful flowers. Then they were back on a very steep, winding road with sharp curves but were able to find a place flat enough to camp at the bottom, surrounded by mountains. The night was warm and restful. Mileage on the truck was 10,208.

A small earthquake jolted them the next morning as they awoke to blistering heat. Once on the road they undertook a terrific descent of sharp, winding curves and were rewarded with an exhilarating view of the ocean. Beautiful desert flowers and cactus blossoms all the way down to the shore presented a resplendent display of all colors and shades---white, yellow, purple, pink, wine, red. Down at the water they roamed over the rocky beach intending to eat lunch there but were discouraged by swarms of biting horseflies. So they ate in the truck and drove on into *La Serena*, a lovely town on a big bay. A large cement plant at the edge of town probably accounted for the cement road they were on for a brief period. *La Serena* marks the southern edge of the Atacama, so from there the landscape became more mountainous and semi-desert with delightful spring flowers. Soon after dark they saw the bright lights of *Ovalle* below them and descended into the city. At the edge of town a man and a little boy were given a ride across one of several rivers that had to be forded to get into the city and out again. The road climbed once more as they left *Ovalle* and, before getting too high, they selected a camping spot in a farm area of flat fields. Santiago: 200 miles away.

Friday, October 1. They woke up to a man pounding on the truck door, presumably the owner of the field. Once they got started, the road took them again into some high mountains that required several stops to cool the radiator. At a gas stop in *Combarbola* they picked up a little boy who wanted to ride 5 km. with them; he sat on Marie's lap with his head in her face. Gas was US¢8/gal. Their next stop was *Illapel* which Eileen described as *"too nice a town for us to be seen in"*. This comment reflected the toll this trip had exacted on the self-esteem of the travelers. For lack of funds, they had been reduced nearly to the status of beggars. Not only had they benefitted from the kindness of strangers, they had come to depend on it and even expect it. At the *Maria Elena* mine they were annoyed when the club charged them for drinks. At *Copiapo* Mr. Holland had bought them food at the market, and they resented the fact that he let them pay for their own ice cream. Marie had a sob story that she told to gain sympathy from truck drivers to get them to buy treats, and they were unhappy whenever it failed to work. Without financial assistance from John and the benevolent folks at *Tacna*, they would have ended in dire straits long before this. Also their plan to finance their return trips to the States by selling the vehicles was now in jeopardy because they had to sell the truck to retrieve the car. That night they camped in a very comfortable spot, surrounded by bushes, 14 miles north of *Los Vilos*. Santiago: 119 miles away.

Saturday was Jan's 25th birthday, a pleasant balmy day with a light fog to filter the sunlight. They ate the last of their oatmeal and corn flakes for breakfast and drove on into *Los* Vilos, a very appealing small port and fishing village. Babe fell in love with the town, perched as it was high on a cliff above a bay resembling that at *San Juan del Sur*. As they drove to *Quilimari* there were frequent views of the ocean and rocky cliffs. At several points they could see construction of the new Roosevelt Highway along the coast with completion scheduled for 1950. They looked for a place to buy bread in *Guaquen;* finding none they searched for a smoking beehive oven but when they found one the bread wasn't done yet. Their search was rewarded in *Quinquimo* but the bread was dry, hard, and tasteless, so they ate canned tuna and sardines just outside the town and watched a parade of men wearing big hats and handsome ponchos (*wassells*) passing by on well-padded saddles on good-looking horses. Each rider had a dog and some men were leading rider-less horses; they were presumed to be coming from a horse sale. The cities were now closer together, mostly pleasant resort towns, the people clean and nicely dressed. *Papudo* was situated on one of the best beaches in Chile and displayed a lot of attractive homes. From there the road curved along the coastline to *Zapallar* with even more delightful homes, many with gorgeous flowers in the yards. Now there was one town after the other: two miles to *Cachagua*, then ten miles inland to *Puchuncavi*. They stopped there for water and an oddly-dressed

man came running over and gave them a map and signal cards. It was cold and storming when they got to *Concón* and, since it was Saturday night, the stores were open; butcher shops with tantalizing meat, restaurants offering a dazzling array of entrees. They were starving but, with only $3 among them, they left with their mouths watering, drove along the ocean, and camped at a pull-off place along the cliffs. Jan's birthday was celebrated with a can of salmon, but their misery was mitigated by a fantastic view of the lights of *Viña del Mar* and *Valparaiso* spread out before them. Santiago: 58 miles away.

The group attracted quite a lot of attention from passers-by next morning. Four young cyclists stopped to chat, a man with a small girl stopped to see Alfredo, a motorcyclist almost had an accident gawking at them. It was a delightful day and a lovely drive along the ocean to *Viña del Ma*r, a highly fashionable resort town with huge stylish homes, awesome hotels, attractive restaurants, and them with only a can of dried peaches for lunch. In driving around town, they were impressed by the Miramar Hotel (right on the water, fine-looking and modern), the Hotel O'Higgins, the Casino, the presidential summer residence (*Castillo Presidencial*) on Castle Hill, and by the city itself: "*a beautiful beach resort*". Six miles around the water and up a hill into *Valparaiso* and oh, what a contrast! The whole hill was a mass of slums, filthy and patched together with scraps. They followed a bus down into the heart of *Valparaiso*, a major seaport, drove along the waterfront, past the harbor area, then up to the main street. Every place was closed because it was Sunday, but they found a bakery that had delicious sweet rolls. Leaving town, the road made a terrific climb up atop the mountains where the terrain resembled the north woods; trees of all descriptions with lots of big pine trees. Later the countryside became very hilly and green with plowed fields and truck gardens, a huge difference from the desert they had just left behind. Then about twenty miles out of *Santiago* they popped through a pass and a breathtaking view of the snow-capped Andes Mountains to the east appeared. The road now dropped down into a thriving green valley where crops of all kinds were being raised. They decided it was too late to drive on into *Santiago*. A farmer gave them permission to camp in his field where they ate sardine sandwiches amid a field of mooing cows. It was an ideal night with a sliver of a moon.

Chapter 23: Santiago

<u>Monday, October 4</u>. It was noon when they arrived in the city. The truck mileage was 10,730. The first stop was at the embassy to get the mail of which there was a ton. There was a note from John. They found him at the Bidart Hotel, a small, clean, old place in the heart of town. He was rooming with a friend, Arturo Echeverria, whom he had met on the plane from *Arica*. The group decided to stay at the Bidart themselves since the rate was only 106 pesos (about US$1.70) a day and that included three meals. They had a six-course lunch that left them popping full  after the meager rations they had been on. The rest of the afternoon was spent reading their mail and unloading things from the truck and into their rooms. People on the street stared at them because of their many suitcases and their strange garb; the girls were wearing slacks. Dinner was a five-course meal that left them satiated and ready to sleep in a bed for only the second night since August 28th when they had just left Lima, Peru.

The next day was spent leisurely with late breakfasts and massages in the morning. A hotel employee tried to take Alfredo out of his cage and was scratched and seriously bitten. After lunch the girls went back to the embassy and were told that it would be difficult to sell the cars and get jobs without permanent visas; also that they had been ripped off badly by all the fees, paperwork, and nuisances that they had encountered at the border. After leaving the embassy they started a half-hearted search for Marie's cousin who was working for an American company in Santiago, but without more specific information about his location they gave up the search and returned to the hotel. The evening was spent playing cards, walking, and people-watching. John and Arturo took Pic and Jan to a movie.

Desperate for some money, on Wednesday Persh sold his razor for 1000 pesos (US$15). They went to see Mr. Trabucco who was Canape's attorney in *Santiago*. He wasn't in, so they made an appointment to see him at 11 a.m. the next day. That appointment became postponed until 5 p.m. the next day. John introduced them to Jorge, who worked in the traffic control tower at the airport. Jorge accompanied them to the embassy to get their paperwork reviewed.

Michael Sumar in Cuzco had encouraged them to visit the Sumar factory at *Santiago*. On Thursday, not knowing what to expect, they rode a bus quite a distance out of town and met Joe Sumar, Michael's cousin, who greeted them warmly and took them on a tour of their new factory only a year old. It was a very large place that included even a modern housing project for their employees. Joe showed them through the whole process from receiving raw cotton in bales from Texas, converting it to fiber, and weaving it into cloth. Everything was done by modern machinery, so new that all the looms hadn't even been set up yet. They met Ray Dumas, an American whose job it was to get all the machinery up and running. Joe's brother César drove them back into town in the company station wagon. Ray Dumas asked the girls to dinner on Friday night, and Joe invited them for Saturday night.

They were 15 minutes late for their appointment with Trabucco who seemed interested in buying the cars. He looked at the truck and liked it but, instead of making an offer, he asked them to set the price they wanted. They were thinking of US$7,500 for both vehicles but decided to wait before making a decision. At Trabucco's office they met his associates, Hugh St. Marie and Ernest Hill, who interpreted for them. Ernest took them to his office and showed them photos of their three farms, *Los Vilas Inc.*, where they raised sheep----30,000 of them. They all adjourned to the City Hotel bar and indulged in *Cuba Libras*. Everyone was a little tipsy as they traipsed back to the Bidart Hotel babbling in Spanglish all the way. Hugh made a date with Marie for dinner and with Marie and Jan to go the horse races on Sunday. Persh and Eileen invited Ernest to dinner, but he declined so they went to see Bogart and Bacall in "Dark Passage".

A conference was held the next morning in which they decided to ask $7500 for the two cars. Trabucco seemed stunned when he heard their offer and refused to discuss the matter further but agreed to do all he could to help get the car down from *Arica* for them. They decided to rethink their asking price. Eileen cabled friends in Janesville asking them to wire some money. At the hotel restaurant, they were introduced to two food items that were new to them: yogurt and artichokes. John and Arturo took Pic and Jan out again and Marie went out with Hugh.

Saturday, October 9. John and Arturo flew to Buenos Aires for a week. Persh, Marie, and Babe went to the garage and spent most of the day retrieving things from the truck. Alfredo got out of his cage and terrified the maid; the staff considered him vicious after he bit the boy.

On Monday, Marie and Babe went window-shopping, looking at displays of silver and copper items. Prices of objects made from both metals were higher than in Peru but still quite a lot cheaper than in the States. Marie thought the Chilean silver seemed heavier and had a brighter finish than Peruvian silver, but it cost more. At the hotel, the group had another conference in which they decided to continue their stay at the Bidart at least for the time being. At their next meeting with Trabucco, he seemed to have changed his mind about how much he could help them. Marie said the discussion went around in circles leaving them confused about what their options were and what role Trabucco was willing to play. The only thing decided was that they would write to Mr. Canape in *Tacna* and ask him to release the car which, if he did so, would be out of the kindness of his heart, trusting them to repay the loan without holding the car as security. Trabucco told them that the import duty had gone up 100% that day, but they later learned that wasn't true. Pic went to dinner with him; Jan and Marie had dates with Caesar and Fernando Sumar. They went to dinner at *Establesimiento Oriente*. Marie said both fellows were interesting conversationalists. She thought they were going dancing as a group, but *"Caesar had plans up his sleeve. He took me riding around town in his convertible, then parked. The little dickens gave me a hard time but wasn't*

too hard to handle. He thinks I look like Gene Tierney. Home at 2:30 a.m.".
Ernest went to dinner with Persh and Eileen at the hotel. Afterwards he
taught them how to play Baccarat and stayed until 2 a.m., seeming reluctant
to leave, as if he wanted to tell them something or was afraid to go home
alone.

Tuesday, October 12. It was Columbus Day and most places were closed so
they walked to the zoo located halfway up San Cristobal Hill. It was a
very fine zoo with many animals and birds including a giant condor. On
their way home, they were drawn to a large crowd of people at a bridge.
There were five men living under the bridge talking, singing, and one
pounding on a big tin can with sticks. Their little inside joke was that the
men were foretelling how six Americans would be living two months in the
future.

On Wednesday, Persh and Pic went to the General Motors agency and
were told that the car should be worth 300,000 pesos and the truck
anywhere from 200,000 to 400,000 pesos. At the lower value for the truck,
the total would have been about US$7,500. In the meantime Marie and
Babe had somehow managed to locate Marie's cousin, Jim Glenn, from
Kansas and showed up at the hotel with him in tow. Jim was an
electrical engineer working for Electromat, a division of General Electric.
He was driving his company's station wagon and took everyone to dinner
at an enjoyable German restaurant. Jim had been a radio operator (Sparks)
on U.S. Merchant Marine ships during the war. One ship he was on got
separated from its convoy in a bad storm, was torpedoed and sunk by a U-
Boat. The crew took to life rafts and was rescued by a British corvette.

Chapter 24: Biding Time in Santiago

The primary concern over the next several weeks was selling the cars. Living without money severely constrained their activities during this period. On October 22, Marie moved out of the hotel to live with her cousin Jim, his wife Mary, and their dogs. The Glenns had a spacious apartment in *Las Condes,* a convenient suburb, and a little Austin that was available for Marie to drive. She was hardest hit by the lack of funds; she had the smallest kitty in the cash pool as she had contributed little or nothing to the purchase of the car but had put in a lot of sweat equity on the turkey farm. Persh and Eileen could get money wired from home with which they helped out the other members of their family. Marie's dad was able to send her an occasional $20 bill.

Pic and Jan ran their own campaign to sell the vehicles. They went to see a lawyer named Lucho who referred them to a potential buyer. Nothing came of that contact, but Lucho became helpful in other ways. He provided notary service, advice on how to deal with Chile's rules and regulations, walked them through the process of applying for permanent visas and, most importantly, offered the girls the use of a small, vacant house that he owned in *Los Vertientes,* a small ski suburb about twenty miles southeast of *Santiago.* The house was actually a garage that Lucho had converted into a ski-house. Pic, Jan, and Babe moved out there on December 18 and remained until they left Chile.

Eileen interviewed for several jobs and was eventually hired as a stenographer for Mr. Robinson, an English importer of textile machinery. She started work on December 2 at a salary of 3500 pesos/month (about US$52) transcribing English shorthand; another secretary handled the Spanish correspondence. Although work interfered with the vagabond lifestyle they had become accustomed to, she stuck it out until she and Persh were nearly ready to leave the country. Persh went through the motions of finding a job but concentrated his efforts on selling the automobiles and planning the next leg of the journey that he and Eileen would take.

The girls were popular with the local men and had no problem finding escorts to take them to a range of social activities: horse racing, boxing, nightclubs, dining out. Some activities were free or inexpensive and they could do them on their own: sightseeing, museums, movies, art galleries, and the zoo. The Bidart was a popular gathering place where people dropped in without notice and stayed to all hours. Without question the most popular activity was partying at the hotel. Fellows would bring wine, champagne, pisco, beer, Scotch, rum, local brews. One night a group of five people consumed five bottles of champagne. The parties would often last past 2:00 a.m. If other hotel guests complained of the noise, they'd be invited to the party.

An important event that passed nearly unnoticed by them was the U. S. presidential election on November 2 that pitted Dewey vs. Truman. There was more interest and excitement about it among the locals than with the travelers who only heard a day or two later that Truman had won but were unaware of the drama at home in which Dewey had been predicted to win.

They participated in local events, the most notable being the Spring Festival held on November 21. On the previous evening, there was a parade of floats down Bernardo O'Higgins Blvd. They all donned weird costumes and joined the revelers in the street. Persh caused quite a sensation dressed in long underwear, open in the rear exposing a black bathing suit underneath, wearing his flying jacket, gauntlets, boots, and a black mask. The next day they hopped onto a passing float and rode it four or five miles to the Stadium (*Estadio Nacional*). The route was lined with mobs of people. Inside, the stadium was aglow with colorful lights, people dancing anywhere and everywhere, floats circling around. There was a boogie-woogie band with people jitterbugging; in another area folks were dancing the Raspa. It was a very colorful, happy atmosphere.

They also attended some national and city celebrations. In December, they went to an affair at the Army Stadium to honor a local young man, Georges de Giorgio, who was going off to the Antarctic. At age 17 he had joined an American expedition to Antarctica becoming the youngest person ever to spend a year there. Now at age 20 he was returning with a Chilean support group to try to claim a share of the Antarctic for Chile. During one of his trips, he lived for a month alone on the Palmer Peninsula plateau and was the first to cross the Antarctic from Atlantic to Pacific by dogsled. Di Giorgio Mountain was named after him. Georges was staying at the Bidart; as fellow adventurers, he and Persh became acquainted.

By Christmas, the group was quite split up. Marie had gone to live with Jim and Mary Glenn in *Las Condes*, the other girls had moved to *Los Vertientes,* and Persh and Eileen had moved into an apartment that served as a focal point for their get-togethers and occasional group activities.

The travelers were pleasantly surprised by the city of *Santiago*. Expecting it might be a provincial capital providing limited exposure to the outside world, they found it to be a very cosmopolitan city in which they, as Americans, felt quite comfortable. After she had moved out to her cousin's place, Marie wrote her impression of *Santiago* in a letter to Don Matting, the artist from Milwaukee: "*Santiago is progressive, modern, with restaurants, ice cream parlors, mountain resorts. Has street cars & trolley-buses, a funicular running up to the top of San Cristobal Hill. Population: 900,000. People are the same descent as us, dress like us, seem to act the same but can tell we're foreigners. The people here are combinations of European races but nearly everyone has some Spanish blood in them. The women are very pretty, but there are hardly any good looking men; however, they make up for that with their personalities. We're trying to learn Spanish and make social contacts so we can sell the cars. I've seen nearly everything in Santiago except the tourist "musts". I've never suffered from boredom even though we are quite isolated out here in the country with no telephone. We have a clear view of the Andes; you should capture the beauty of their snow-capped peaks in the evening in a watercolor. Much is to be said for the country clubs, nightclubs, theaters, restaurants, shops, summer resorts, horse races, casinos, wines, and climate. All in all, Chile is OK---it has been wonderful for a visit, but give me the States. None of us know what we're going to do upon arriving back, but the four of us will be centered in the Madison area. Persh and Eileen will stay here for a while before extending their trip to some other part of South America".*

The City of Santiago
October 1948

Chapter 25: Selling the Cars

They had to sell the truck to get enough money to repay the loan on the bond and the import duties on both vehicles. At first they depended on word-of-mouth advertising among their few acquaintances which resulted in some looky-loos but no offers. In early December they ran an ad in the newspaper but had no response. They ran the ad again and only one person, Mr. Brunswell, responded. Two days later he called to say he

wanted to buy the truck, and the deal was closed on Christmas Eve. He paid 90,000 pesos in cash and a check for 170,000 pesos payable on January 5 but deducted 1,600 pesos for repairs to the dented fender. They promptly sent 57,000 pesos to George Koch in *Arica* to release the car. So they netted 201,400 pesos, equivalent to US$3,000.

On January 7, 1949, Persh flew up to *Arica* to get the car. He returned to *Santiago* on Jan. 21 with a very dirty vehicle. He was forced to wait two days for a river to recede before he could ford it, then spent two days in *Antofagasta* getting necessary repairs made. On February 3, the car was sold to a dealer for 300,000 pesos (US$4,500). They had paid $1,750 for it when they bought it in Janesville.

They were all vastly relieved to get the money for the vehicles since they had been pinching pennies just to get by long before they arrived in *Santiago* in October. Marie wrote: *"now we're rolling in dough---pesos, that is, and with the exchange rate at nearly 70 pesos to the dollar we're beginning to carry satchels instead of purses (just kidding). It's a nice feeling. We've been very fortunate in that now we at least have enough money to tear ourselves away from this country."*

Chapter 26: Relationships

Eileen kept meticulous notes on details in her diary: miles and kilometers, elevation heights, what was for sale in the markets, how much things cost, food purchased and eaten, places where they camped, but she seldom mentioned the human interactions and relationships that add spice and flavor to travel. Marie described the trip more in terms of her personal experiences. Yet wherever they went, they encountered kindhearted and caring people with whom real bonds of friendship and affection were formed: Jesse and Manuel in *Oaxaca*; Herbert Allisat and his mother in El Salvador; The GIs: Smokey, Herb, Ben and Ed in Honduras; Henrique in *Mejorada*. The amazing folks in *Rivas*: the doctor and Johnny; Eugene Maurice who gave them a house, provided them with food, and proposed marriage to Pic; Alfredo Urcayo who gave Babe the monkey; Taversé, the handy-lady next door; Mr. Holmann at *San Juan del Sur* who made everything possible for them; Michael Sumar in *Cuzco* and his cousins, Joe and César, in *Santiago*; Elisa and Max at *Tacna;* Lucho who befriended the girls in *Santiago*. How fortunate they were to encounter such marvelous, kind, and helpful people. Eileen did admit that *"if there is any one thing we'll never forget about our trip, it is the wonderful people we found wherever we went."* Marie also commented that *"wherever we go we meet many nice people who are extremely friendly and hospitable"*. In fact, the one great sustaining element of their journey was the friendliness and helpfulness of the people they met along the way. Someone was always ready to help them.

There was also a sub-current of sentiment and romance associated with the girls who attracted men wherever they went. Marie seemed to receive a disproportionate share of that attention which at times caused a bit of jealousy from her two friends. Perhaps it was because she fit easily into the Latin culture with her dark hair and skin that bronzed readily in the tropical sun. Along with her natural beauty, she seemed at ease in all kinds of social situations, and the way she intermingled her attempts at speaking

Spanish with the smattering of Italian she had picked up in Rome came across as charming. Especially charmed were the two men of the Rivas family: the 55-year old father and the 22-year old son.

When the travelers arrived at the American Embassy in Santiago on October 4, there was a letter addressed to Marie from Dr. Alfonso Rivas. It read in part: "*My dearest Marie. My life has been so lonely since you left. I think of you every day and wish that you were here beside me. When I am got myself in my Ranch or in some other places where we were together, I miss you so very much. I worry that you may meet with harm on the road or that you may be in a place needing help. How I wish that you would return to Nicaragua and come to live with us. I would like to take care of you and keep you from all worries. I send my deepest affection.*" Marie responded with a letter the next day. In it she told Dr. Rivas how touched she was by his kind comments, how thankful they all were for everything that he had done for them, that she had wonderful memories of their times together, that she felt a strong love for him and his family, but she was eager to return to Wisconsin where she had a boyfriend and was contemplating marriage in the near future. He replied on Nov. 7: "*I cannot thank you enough for your kindness thought you had mentioned conserned (sic) to my family and myself. I am very glad to know that you arrived at Santiago O.K. I would like to know when you are planning to leave for U.S.A. or are you going to stay in Santiago for a considerable time? Please excuse me for not writing much. It is not because I have nothing to say but because I feel like to see you than write. And don't forget that this place of mine is yours too. With many good kisses. Signed: A. A. Rivas.*"

Johnny had fallen for Marie at first sight, and during the extended stay of the group in Nicaragua he became deeply enamored. Feeling lonely and nearly heartbroken after the *Santa Fe* sailed from *San Juan del Sur*, he traveled to the U.S. as scheduled, leaving Nicaragua just a week later. He traveled by land, sight-  seeing and visiting along the way. He entered the U.S. from Mexico at Laredo, Texas, on September 8, 1948, and finally arrived in Denver on December 19. He had only $30 in his pocket because a new regime in

Nicaragua wouldn't permit money to be taken out of the country. But he soon found a job in a hospital operating room. He already had quite a few credits toward medical school from Nicaragua, so he applied to twenty American universities for admission and received only one favorable reply, from Syracuse University. But he was admitted to and graduated from the University of Colorado Medical School. On March 6, 1949, he wrote Marie from Denver: *"I have had some dates with girls here (they like the way I talk) but I don't feel happy. I go out with a girl once or twice and I get tired of her. Is a big difference when I was with you. That was wonderful and unparalleled. I will never forget you. I think your remember will accompany me the rest of my life, that I want to be long, because then I will enjoy remembering those times of big happiness that I had with you. I can't forget the walks in the beach with you, the moon and the palms and our love feeling the tropic magic. Maybe this looks silly to you because is not U.S. way, but is not my fault that you came so dip in my heart. I remember all and each one of the moments we had together. I now (sic) that we are not a Romeo and Juliet. Those things are just in books and films. The reality of life is different. We can't have everything we want. Such is life. The times that shall come no more. But remember this: I LOVE YOU. Signed: Johnny"*.

Johnny never saw Marie again. In the mid-1950s he was listed as a resident physician at the State Hospital at Pueblo, Colorado. In 1959 he was living in Norman, Oklahoma. He visited Pic and Jan in Janesville at some point during this time. On Jan 15, 1960, he married Elia Margarita Cantu Gonzalez in Cuatro Cienegas de Carranza, Coahuila, Mexico. The marriage was recorded in Nicaraguan civil records at Rivas, Nicaragua, on August 7, 1968. No records of his later history were found, but it is believed that he returned to Nicaragua to live in 1968, exactly twenty years after his sorrowful departure.

Chapter 27: Going Home

The troop that had gathered in Santiago in October, 1948, left Chile at different times and for different destinations.

On February 24, 1949, Pic, Jan, Marie, and Babe boarded the *Reina del Pacifico*, a luxury passenger ship that sailed regularly between *Valparaiso* and Liverpool, England. Their third class fare to Havana, Cuba, was 6,240 pesos (about $100). Lorito, the parrot, accompanied them. They arrived in Havana on March 10. There they ran into trouble with a local taxi driver who became so frustrated he dumped them off at a police station. They were actually placed in a prison cell but were soon released after Pic created a scene and threatened to call the U. S. Embassy. On March 12, they traveled by boat to Miami. On March 16, Pic, Jan, and Babe took the bus back to Janesville. Back home, Babe returned to her hobby and part-time profession of antiquing. She passed away there at the age of 63 in June 1959. Pic and Jan started a small business making and selling pies in Janesville (JAN AND PIC HOMEMADE PIES). Pies were sold over-the-counter to walk-in customers but their main business was in supplying area restaurants. It was so successful that it taxed their ability to manage it, so after three years they sold out. Still obsessed with wanderlust, they traveled around the states visiting friends and working at temporary jobs to support their travels. In Reno, they were hired by a casino to play the house's money to gamble and attract customers. In 1955, they went to a friend's wedding in Bogota, Colombia, and stayed for two years. On their way back they flew into Houston, Texas, where they found jobs in the booming petroleum and real estate industries and settled down for a long stay. Pic died there at age 81 in February 2004 and Jan at age 90 in September 2013. All three of them are buried in the cemetery at Emerald Grove, Wisconsin.

Marie splurged a bit on buying copper and silver items in Chile and was so broke when she arrived in Florida she didn't have bus fare back to Wisconsin. She stayed with Steve's mother in Miami and worked in a dress factory for a few weeks to earn enough to pay for her fare home. In April 1949, just a year after leaving on their trip, she arrived back in Janesville at loose ends. Five months later, on September 17, 1949, she married Henry (Hank) Jaastad from Eau Claire, Wisconsin. They had a daughter, Randine. Hank died in an automobile accident in February 1965. Marie died in Palm Desert, California, in November 2007 at the age of 84. She is buried with Hank at Forest Hill Cemetery in Eau Claire.

Alfredo, the monkey, was shipped by air from Santiago to a chimpanzee farm in Florida on March 15, 1949, where he nearly died of heat stroke when the girls left him in a car after they picked him up. Alfredo stayed with Pic and Jan, Babe, and other relatives in the Janesville area for several years but became more cantankerous as he aged. He was finally donated to the Vilas Park zoo in Madison where he lived out the rest of his life.

Persh and Eileen moved from the Bidart Hotel into an apartment on December 24. On May 27, 1949, they boarded the *Reina del Pacifico* in *Valparaiso*, passed through the Panama Canal on June 5, and disembarked in *Cartagena,* Colombia a day later. They traveled by train and boat inland to *Medellin.* From there they traveled by riverboat back up the Magdalena River, stopping at numerous small backwater towns: *El Banco, Barranca Bermeja, Puerto Wilches,* and many others, looking for wild animals to take back to the States. But instead of hunting for the animals, they shopped for them. On September 30, they were the only human passengers as they carried two live ocelots and two boa constrictors aboard the Rexton Kent, a Canadian banana boat bound from Barranquilla to Miami. Persh sold the snakes there to a shop that specialized in articles made of snake skin. The ocelots were sold to the Vilas Park zoo in Madison. The couple traveled from Miami back to the Midwest by bus, arriving home in Cloverdale, Indiana, on Oct. 12. Eileen hated to leave Florida for the north *"where it is dirty and cold. I don't know why anyone lives in the north unless it is because they have husbands like mine who can't wait to get back to Cloverdale."* Persh was indeed excited and relieved to arrive home, but for Eileen it was a big letdown as she reminisced about their exciting adventures and remembered how dull small towns such as Cloverdale could be. She took a job with American States Insurance in Indianapolis and was later transferred to Southern California where she died at age 91 in November 2009 in Santa Ana where her remains were cremated. She and Persh were amicably divorced in 1965. Persh returned to farming and trapping but broke the monotony with an occasional hunting trip. He returned to Nicaragua to hunt in 1954 and became involved in an international incident (see Footnote #15). He died in Cloverdale in March 2009 at the age of 90. He is buried with the rest of the Pickens family in the cemetery at Emerald Grove, Wisconsin.

So ended the saga of their journey on the road too far. Too far from home. Too far from comfort. Too far with no money. Too far while being hungry, going without sleep, being too cold, too hot. Too far with no alternative but to carry on. But every road has an end, and at long last they completed their journey on this road that had challenged them so often and so relentlessly. They had braved it through, overcome their unanticipated hardships, and succeeded in their ultimate goal. It was an amazing adventure that no one else would ever experience, one that would shape the rest of their lives.

THE END

FOOTNOTES

[1] In 1717, the valley had 3,000 residents, a pious group of which petitioned the Spanish colonial government, based in Guatemala, for status as a *villa* (village). On May 29, 1720, the request was granted and the name *La Villa de la Pura y Limpia Concepción de Nuestra Señora la Virgen Maria* was approved by the *Capitania General de Guatemala, Francisco Rodriguez de Rivas*. To honor him, the villagers had the name changed to *La Villa de la Pura y Limpia Concepción de Rivas de Nicaragua* which translates to 'The Village of the Immaculate Conception of Rivas of Nicaragua', (an unlikely event). On May 20, 1835, the village was elevated to the status of city and the name shortened to Rivas. At that time, the haciendas grew cocoa for chocolate, corn, beans, and plantain. The most prominent citizen, Don Silvio Guzman, had a large plantation of cocoa including several thousand cocoa houses where the beans were fermented and dried.

[2] Monterrey had a population of about 350,000 in 1948 and is the ninth largest city in Mexico. It is considered to be the most Americanized city in Mexico. It is also one of the wealthiest cities in Mexico, being heavily industrialized and home to many companies, both foreign and domestic.

[3] The Tropic of Cancer is the most northerly circle of latitude on earth at which the sun can be directly overhead. This occurs in June, when the northern hemisphere is tilted toward the sun to its maximum extent. Its southern hemisphere counterpart, marking the most southerly position at which the sun can be directly overhead, is the Tropic of Capricorn. The area between these two zones is defined as tropical.

[4] The Huasteca are an indigenous people of Mexico, living in the La Huasteca region including the states of Hidalgo, Veracruz, San Luis Potosí and Tamaulipas. The ancient Huastec civilization is one of the pre-Columbian Mesoamerican cultures, thought to date back to approximately the 10th century BC. The pre-Columbian Huastecs constructed temples on

i

step-pyramids, carved independently standing sculptures, and produced elaborately painted pottery. They were admired for their abilities as musicians by other Mesoamerican peoples. About 1450, the Huastecs were defeated by Aztec armies under the leadership of Moctezuma I; the Huastecs henceforth paid tribute to the Aztec Empire but retained a large degree of local self-government. They were conquered by the Spanish between 1519 and the 1530s. After the Spanish Conquest, many Huastecs were sold as slaves in the Caribbean by the Spanish.

[5] Lake Texcoco (*Lago de Texcoco*) was a natural lake within the "Anahuac" or Valley of Mexico. It is best known as being the place where the Aztecs built the city of Tenochtitlan, which was located on an island within the lake. After the Spanish conquest of the Aztec Empire, efforts to control flooding by the Spanish led to most of the lake being drained. The entire lake basin is now almost completely occupied by Mexico City.

[6] People generally associate Puebla with the birthplace of the Mexican Revolution, as well as the site of the battle of Cinco de Mayo. *Los Secretos de Puebla*, a series of tunnels connecting the city to the military fortress, were used by the Mexican Army to defeat the French in the famous battle.

[7] Cortez is alleged to have murdered his wife, and the mountain is named *La Malinche* after a native woman who had been sold as a slave to the Spanish conquistadores and helped Cortez as his interpreter during his conquest of the Aztecs. She also bore him a son.

[8] The Tree of Tule, a bald cypress, is perhaps the most famous giant tree in the world. What General Grant is to sequoias, *El Arbor del Tule* is to the bald cypress. It grows at an elevation of 5,100 ft. six miles outside the city of Oaxaca, surrounded by a neatly manicured lawn, flowerbeds, and a wrought iron fence. It is so large it was originally thought to be multiple trees but DNA tests prove it to be a single tree. Its age is unknown; estimates range between 1,200 and 3,000 years. Local legend claims it was planted 1,400 years ago by Pecocha, an Aztec priest, which is in broad agreement with the best scientific estimate.

[9] *Monte Albán* is a large pre-Columbian archaeological site located about six miles west of the city of Oaxaca. It was founded about 800 BC and served as the center of the Zapotec Indian culture for about 1000 years. It was largely abandoned by the Zapotecs around 750 AD but was taken over by the Mixtecs. The site is characterized by several hundred artificial terraces, and a dozen clusters of mounded architecture covering the entire ridge which stands about 1300 ft. above the valley floor.

[10] *Tehuantepec* is the center of Zapotec culture. Eileen was told that the name means "Mountain of the Man Eaters" because hills behind the town were said to be infested with man-eating beasts. Another more likely version calls it "wild animal hill", the name given to the area by the Aztecs, purportedly because of the ferocity of the native Zapotec warriors they encountered there. The city is known for its women and their traditional dress, which was adopted by Frida Kahlo. *Tehuantepec* has a reputation for being a "matriarchal society." Women do dominate the local markets and are known to taunt men.

[11.] Lake Atitlan, seven miles long at an elevation of 5,125 ft. with a surface area of 50.23 mi^2 lies in a massive volcanic crater. It is known for its Mayan villages and volcanoes with sharp pointed cones. The busy town of *Panajachel*, where vendors sell traditional textiles, is a popular gateway to the lake.

[12.] Santa Domingo Church and Monastery dates back to 1538 but was reduced to ruins by an earthquake in 1773. Some excavation was begun in 1941.

[13]. San Francisco el Grande was built in the 16th century. It has suffered seismic damage since its beginning. In 1565 the first building was severely damaged and the tremors continued until 1773. After being abandoned for almost two hundred years, the church was rebuilt in 1961-67 when the Franciscans recovered the property. It has been open for Catholic worship ever since.

[14.] Lake Nicaragua, 92 miles long and 34 miles wide, is said to be the only freshwater lake having sharks in it. It drains to both the Caribbean and the Pacific Ocean via the *San Juan* River. There is an active double volcano, Ometepe, that forms an island in the middle of the lake.

14-A. William Walker was an American mercenary who tried to establish control of Mexico and Central America and convert them to slave-holding, English-speaking colonies. He set himself up as President of Nicaragua through a fraudulent election in 1856. His army was defeated in a battle at *Rivas* by a coalition of Central American states, but his defeated soldiers burned the city of *Granada* to the ground and poisoned the water at *Rivas* by throwing corpses in all the wells as they fought their way back to Lake Nicaragua where they took temporary refuge in William Walker's schooner.

15. Persh's return to the Costa Rican border in November, 1954, created an international incident. The following article was published in the Indianapolis Star in January, 1955.

"Military authorities in strife-torn Costa Rica last night held two Hoosier big game hunters who made a wrong turn in the jungle while stalking cougars. Pershing C. Pickens, 36 years old, and Jack E. Swope, 27, both of Cloverdale, Indiana, were forced to cancel their two-man safari when they stumbled headlong into a war. U. S. Embassy officials at San Jose, Costa Rica, said Pickens and Swope were being guarded by government troops at Upala, a village of 100 population in wild jungle country on the Zapote River below the eastern tip of Lake Nicaragua. Pickens and Swope crossed into invasion-plagued Costa Rica from Nicaragua, evidently not aware of the war situation, four days ago. A Costa Rica patrol, suspicious of strangers in the tension-filled border zone, detained them because they lacked the necessary travel documents. Pickens notified the U.S. Embassy at San Jose by telegraph and gave The Indianapolis Star as a reference. The Star late yesterday reached United States officials at San Jose by radiotelephone and confirmed the identities of the Indiana men to speed their release. Allan Stewart, first secretary of the American embassy in Costa Rica, said the Hoosiers "had never been in Costa Rica before and we didn't have any line on them," The Embassy official said they were being treated well and probably were staying at the Costa Rican commander's headquarters at Upala. He indicated they would be brought to San Jose upon their release instead of being returned to Nicaragua. The outdoorsmen ran afoul of the peppery Central American military uprising about 40 miles and one high mountain range away from the actual combat zone, Stewart said".

[16.] A Carnet is an international customs and temporary export-import document. It is used to clear customs in 87 countries and territories without paying duties and import taxes on merchandise that will be re-exported within 12 months.

[17.] 28th de Julio. A national holiday celebrating the independence of Peru from Spanish colonialism, proclaimed by Jose de San Martin, July 28, 1821 as follows: *DESDE ESTE MOMENTO EL PERÚ ES LIBRE E INDEPENDIENTE POR LA VOLUNTAD GENERAL DE LOS PUEBLOS Y POR LA JUSTICIA DE SU CAUSA QUE DIOS DEFIENDE. ¡VIVA LA PATRIA! ¡VIVA LA LIBERTAD! ¡VIVA LA INDEPENDENCIA!* (From this moment, Peru is free and independent by the general will of the people and by the justice of their cause that God defends. Long Live Peru. Long Live Freedom. Long Live Independence.)

[18.] Gran Hotel Bolivar dedicated on July 28, 1921 to commemorate the 100th anniversary of Peruvian independence.

[19.] Panagra. Pan American-Grace airlines held a near-monopoly over air travel in South America during the 1940s and 1950s. Through a series of mergers and acquisitions, these routes are now flown by American Airlines.

[20.] The Andean cock-of-the-rock (Rupicola peruvianus) (known as tunki in Quechua) is a large passerine bird of the cotinga family native to Andean cloud forests in South America. It is widely regarded as the national bird of Peru.

[21.] *Arica* is Chile's northernmost city, located 11 miles south of the Peruvian border. It is an important port city for a large portion of South America. Rain is virtually unknown and its mild weather and attractive beaches make it known as the "city of eternal spring". An attraction is *Morro de Arica*, a steep and tall hill that was the scene of a historic battle in 1880 when Chilean forces captured it from Peru. There is a nearby oasis where vegetables and olives are grown.

[22.] Aduana is the agency or office that collects the taxes on imported goods

<u>PHOTOS</u>

PIC, JAN, MARIE

BABE

Johnny Rivas   **With Marie**

With a paca   **With the fawn**

Navy Lt. Pershing Pickens

Persh

Persh as Desperado

San Juan del Sur

Eileen with dressed pacas

Rivas

Persh & Eileen

Santiago, Chile

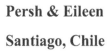

Roadside Pyramid, Guatemala

Back Rooms at the House in Rivas

Jan with octupi

San Juan del Sur

Pic with horse

Rivas Ranch

Pic with native woman

Peru

Dinner at Henriques
Mejorada, Peru
Standing: Persh, Henrique
Seated: Henrique's servant,
Pic, Babe, Eileen, Jan

Bakery cart
Los Vertientes, Chile

MAPS

MEXICO

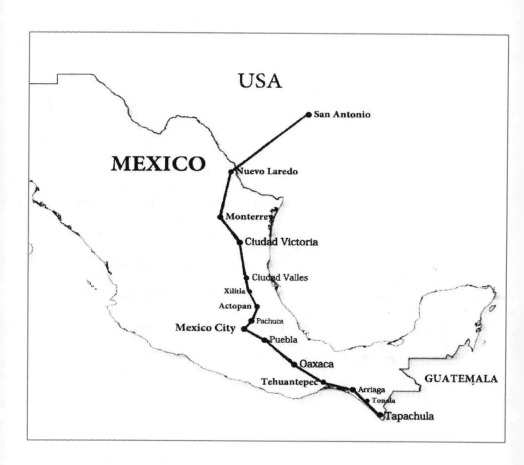

CENTRAL AMERICA

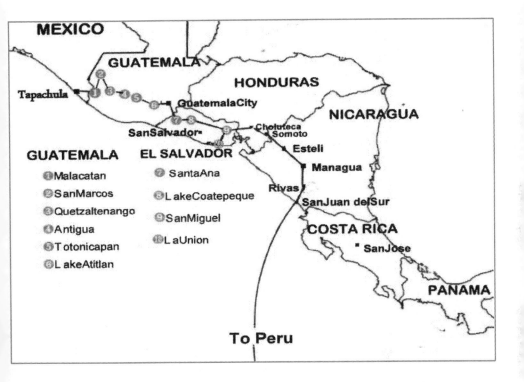

ECUADOR, PERU

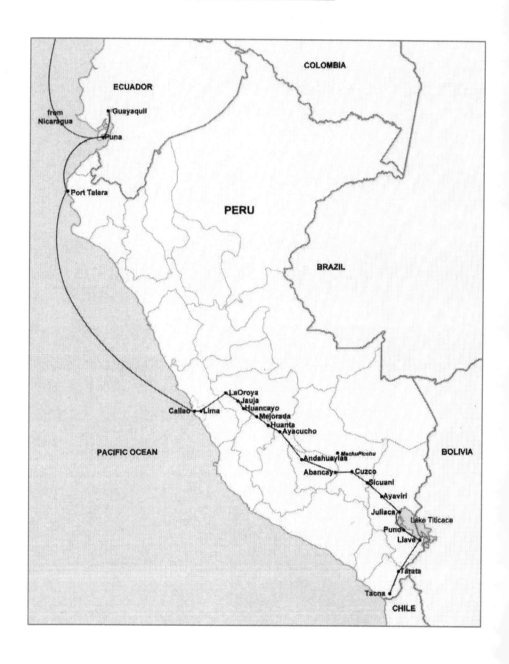

CHILE

Made in the USA
Columbia, SC
07 August 2021